Motorbooks International
WARBIRD HISTORY

# B-24
## LIBERATOR

Frederick A. Johnsen

*For Sharon, who provides
the healthy counterpoint to my
aviation passions.*

First published in 1993 by Motorbooks International Publishers & Wholesalers, PO Box 2, 729 Prospect Avenue, Osceola, WI 54020 USA

Library of Congress Cataloging-in-Publication Data
    Johnsen, Frederick A.
        B-24 Liberator/Frederick A. Johnsen.
        p. cm. — (Warbird history series)
        Includes bibliographical references and index.
    ISBN 0-87938-758-0
        1. B-24 (Bomber) I. Title. II. Series.
    UG1242.B6J6    1993
    358.4'283—dc20          93-1160

Printed in Hong Kong

**On the front cover:** A tiger-faced B-24D with Oklahoma City Modification Center nose-turret conversion splashed color on an otherwise somber olive drab bomber. *US Air Force Museum*

**On the back cover:** Top, a mottled Privateer with the ERCO bow turret. *San Diego Aerospace Museum*. Below, pilot Ted Small's LB–30 *Tiger Lady* of the 6th BG. *Ted Small Collection.*

**On the frontispiece:** *Joy Rider* was a Pacific Privateer. *L. M. Myers Collection*

**On the title page:** Air Force enlisted men relax beside *Tubarão*, the brightly-painted formation ship used by the 491st bomb group in England. Retired from combat, this B-24J received bright markings to aid other 491st BG pilots in locating where to assemble after takeoff for the formation run to the target. The formation assembly ship did not accompany the other B-24s on the mission. *Jeff Ethell collection*

# Contents

# Preface

Understand right from the start, I've been an unabashed fan of Liberators and Privateers since I was a small boy.

It's difficult to analyze these things. Maybe it all started with a childhood fascination with an old Revell B-24J model kit of dubious accuracy. Perhaps it was the "Victory at Sea" footage of the air war in the Pacific, accompanied by the symphonic strains of "Beneath the Southern Cross" as outbound Liberators passed graceful palm trees. However it started, my love of the Liberator was fed by those remarkable *National Geographic* wartime photo stories, and tales of air combat with Messerschmitts related by the genial landlord of the house my family rented in the late 1950s.

As I grew older, I devoured the news accounts of the finding of the B-

*Bent but amazingly intact, the ghostly* Lady Be Good *fired the public's imagination when the lost B-24D was found by oil prospectors in the Libyan desert in 1959. In 1962, the US Air Force invoked its procedure for property disposal by advertising to sell* Lady Be Good *to the highest bidder. There were no takers. US Air Force Museum Collection.*

24D *Lady Be Good* in Libya. Stories about Ploesti gripped my attention. This was high adventure for a boy. But the more I sought out every shred of information about my favorite aircraft, the more I heard stories about the Liberator's supposed inferiorities to the B-17, or how Liberators were unwanted guests in the European Theater of Operations.

And yet, the Liberator had its staunch partisans: crew members who wouldn't let the Lib take a slur in conversation many years after the end of their wartime association with B-24s; historians who extolled the versatility of the Liberator airframe. These voices were raised in defense of this nearly extinct, obsolete heavy bomber.

And therein lies a major reason for my ongoing passion for this airplane—the people who lived and died by it. If early B-24s in the Pacific were not sufficiently defended from head-on attacks, American aviators devised a power turret to remedy the problem, exercising that wonderful Yankee ingenuity found on either side of the Mason-Dixon Line. When the war in Europe and the Middle East was far from a foregone Allied victory, American aviators climbed aboard stout B-24Ds and weaved among smokestacks to bomb

vital oil refineries from rooftop level in a daring mission that was certain to claim many of their lives. When the comforts of home were thousands of miles from the South Pacific, Americans in B-24s brought these comforts a bit closer by taking the necessary ingredients aloft, where atmospheric refrigeration allowed ice cream to be churned high above the steaming tropics. And when paint and brushes were put in the hands of squadron artists, American aviators used the broad flanks of the Liberators and Privateers to create the definitive examples of warplane nose art.

We Americans pride ourselves in having a can-do spirit. That spirit emerges in the tale of the Consolidated B-24 and PB4Y bombers.

Browse with me through Liberator archives in this volume. Sure, we've heard from those who criticized aspects of the B-24, sometimes with good cause. But that only adds depth to the story of the most heavily produced American military plane ever, and the upbeat flight crews, ground crews, support people, and engineers who took the B-24 into battle and emerged victorious.

—*Frederick A. Johnsen*

# Technical Notes

If you've ever worked around a major Air Force aircraft production run, you know that what "the book" says is not always the way it really is. The deeper we delve into the history of more than 18,000 Liberators and Privateers, the more variables we find. Effort has been made to use reliable documentation to explain many quirks and changes in Liberator production. But in the crush of World War II events, some things didn't get done by the book. They didn't even get *entered* in the book. Use the information in this volume as a guide to the wonderful world of B-24s and their kin, but keep light on your feet for anomalies that may still show up in Liberator research. Be wary of anyone who professes to know everything about B-24s, for Liberators were in service in too many arenas at once for anybody to keep an omniscient eye on them all. And friends, with this volume I've uncovered and corrected some errors I, and other writers, inadvertently allowed into print earlier. It is ironic that we get more accurate in some aspects of the complex B-24 story as more years elapse, even as we lose more of the precious first-person memories of the Liberator years each time a veteran dies.

# Acknowledgments

The list of people who have generously helped build my B-24 research files is continually growing. The naming of those who had a hand in the materials presented in this book must start off with Peter M. Bowers, whose unselfish lending of photos from his vast collection provided a meaty nucleus for this book. Thanks, Pete.

Others who have helped, over several decades, include: Rick Apitz, Rhodes Arnold, David Gale Behunin, Steve Birdsall, the Confederate Air Force Museum, Convair-General Dynamics, Jim Dilonardo, Johnny Dingle, Jeff Ethell, Bob Etter, Wayne Fiamengo, Tom Foote, Charlie Glassie, Jr., Chet Goad, A. B. Goldberg, Carl Hildebrandt, William G. Holder, Ben Howser, Albert W. James, Larry Jaynes, Mr. and Mrs. Carl M. Johnsen, Kenneth G. Johnsen, Don Keller, Jim Kiernan and Sharon D. Vance Kiernan, Keith Laird, Fred LePage, the Liberator Club (and especially Bob McGuire), Al Lloyd, Al Lomer, Ray Markman, Jim Masura, Dave Menard, Allan Metscher, Bill Metscher, Bill Miranda, Louis Mladenovic, L. M. Myers, Thomas K. Oliver, Earl Otto, Dennis Peltier, Milo Peltzer, Bob Richardson, Bill Riepl, Rockwell International (and Gene Boswell), the San Diego Aerospace Museum (and Ray Wagner and George Welsh), Walter Schurr, Victor D. Seely, Ted Small, Glen Spieth, Ivan Stepnich, Carl A. Stutz, David Tallichet, Herb Tollefson, Orville Tosch, University of Washington Aeronautical Laboratory (and Professor William H. Rae, Jr.), US Air Force Museum, US Navy office of history, Bill Willard, and Charles F. Willis, Jr.

Documentation compiled since the 1940s by US Air Force historians unlocks riddles, and adds much to the biography of the Liberator. The Air Force can be proud of its half-century of diligent historical record-keeping.

Motorbooks' aviation editor Greg Field fostered this project. I like to think he knows a good thing when he sees one.

## Chapter 1

# Pedigree

### New Ideas

The B-24 Liberator (Consolidated Aircraft Co. Model 32) was that company's reply to a US Army Air Corps suggestion that Consolidated establish a second production line to turn out more Boeing-designed B-17 Flying Fortresses. To speed a mock-up of its own heavy bomber design into readiness for Air Corps inspectors, Consolidated engineers borrowed the untried Davis wing from the Model 31 flying boat proposal, along with the Model 31's huge twin-tail assembly. (The wing was named for its inventor David R. Davis.) In a late-war issue of *Aviation* magazine, J. H. Famme, Consolidated's chief design engineer at San Diego, said, "Ease of production was one of the main considerations in selecting this wing design." According to Famme, the front and rear wing spars were widely spaced "to provide maximum room for fuel cells of sufficient capacity to insure the greater range specified by the Army Air Forces [AAF], and also to provide clearance for main landing gear wheels."

On March 30, 1939, signers inked the contract for a mock-up wind-tunnel model, and one prototype XB-24 airplane. Exactly nine months later to the

day, the XB-24 was supposed to be completed. In actuality, the prototype first took to the air on December 29, 1939, more than a month early.

### The Davis Wing

By the time the XB-24 first left the runway, the Davis wing had flown (on May 5, 1939) on the prototype Model

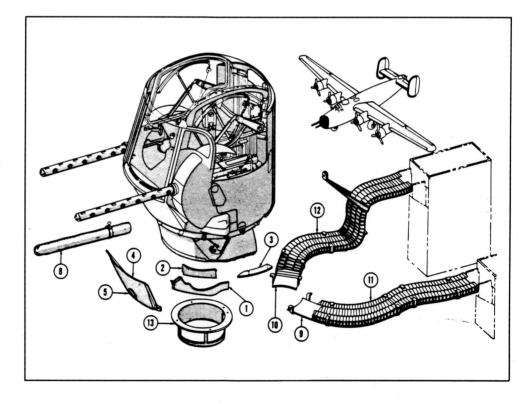

*The oldest surviving Liberator is the LB-30B flown by the Confederate Air Force.* Frederick A. Johnsen

*Motor Products Corp. (MPC) nose and tail turrets refined the basic Consolidated design with streamlining, more glazing, and gently curved armor glass.*

*Gun mounts were symmetrical. Externally mounted ammunition cans fed all the nose and tail turrets.*

*Prototype XB-24 (39-556) set the basic form of all Liberators to follow, even as metamorphosis embellished the line.* Peter M. Bowers Collection

*When fitted with turbo-supercharged versions of the R-1830 engine, and other refinements, the prototype XB-24 was renumbered 39-680, and redesignated XB-24B. A salient feature of the sole B-model was the use of characteristic wide oval nacelles on the stubby airframe of the prototype. Propeller spinners were tested.* San Diego Aerospace Museum

31, and engineers were enthusiastic about the performance edge it gave. Now the B-24's fortunes were tied to the abilities of the Davis high-lift airfoil. Although, as if still not unanimous in their confidence, Consolidated engineers ran a wind-tunnel test on the Davis airfoil only days before the XB-24's first flight. Two wings were compared in this test, in the University of Washington Aeronautical Laboratory (UWAL) wind tunnel, between December 21 and 26. One of the 1/12 scale wings used the Davis airfoil; the other employed a more traditional National Advisory Council on Aeronautics (NACA) 230 series airfoil. Both wing models used the same planform as did the XB-24, and earlier the Model 31, with an aspect ratio of 11.6. This was a high ratio—a feature that minimized some components of drag, contributing to the efficiency of the wing.

The wind-tunnel results showed Davis' wing promoted a laminar airflow over a greater portion of the chord (from leading edge to trailing edge of the wing) than did the NACA section. This gave the Davis wing a lift advantage: Lift increases with an increase in pitch (angle of attack) of the wing, up to the point where the airflow separates from the wing and aerodynamic stall occurs. The data for the Davis wing confirmed that it enjoyed increasing lift at increasingly higher angles of attack up to the stall point with a smaller drag penalty than did the NACA wing.

Perhaps most telling was a graph plotted at airspeeds between 150 and 250mph, and a theoretical altitude of 10,000ft. The graph showed that the Davis wing gave 150mi greater range than did the NACA wing at 150mph, with that benefit dwindling to 40mi extra range for the Davis wing at 240mph. The Davis wing had the range.

As designed, the B-24 wing was intended to incorporate rubber deicer boots that physically altered their shape enough to slough off ice in flight. Later, Convair introduced a new hot-air exhaust heat anti-icing system. The exhaust heat system necessitated ducting and double-skin sections to conduct heated air to the leading edge surfaces. On Liberators so equipped, air heated by exhaust gases was piped through the leading edges of flight surfaces, as well as into the compartments of the pilots, radio operator, bombardier, tail gunner, and top turret. Other crew members still relied on electrically heated clothing. The heat exchangers for this system were located in the engine exhaust stacks just ahead of the turbosuperchargers. Outside air passed through the heat exchangers before flowing through the aluminum tube ducting to locations where needed. The

*Flight-test crew members flashed V-for-Victory signals to mimic that given by* Gran'pappy *painted on the nose of the XB-24B. The first Liberator outlived* the war as a test and transport aircraft, finally being scrapped in 1946. San Diego Aerospace Museum

*Trading on its options, the AAF gave six of its seven ordered YB-24s to the British, to wait for more advanced production Liberators. That makes this the* sole true YB-24, number 40-702. Orthochromatic film altered the appearance of the national star insignia tones. Peter M. Bowers Collection

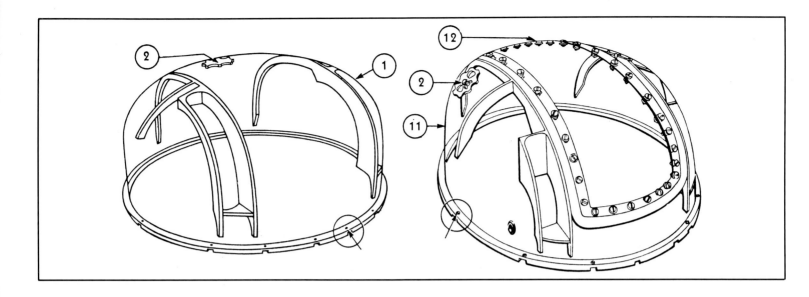

Two types of Martin top-turret Plexiglas domes graced B-24s. Photographs taken well into J-model and Privateer production still show the old-style dome (left). When the K-13 and other computing gunsights were introduced, the dome was redesigned with a replaceable center Plexiglas sighting window with a constant-radius curvature to facilitate accurate sighting. This resulted in the so-called "high hat" dome (right).

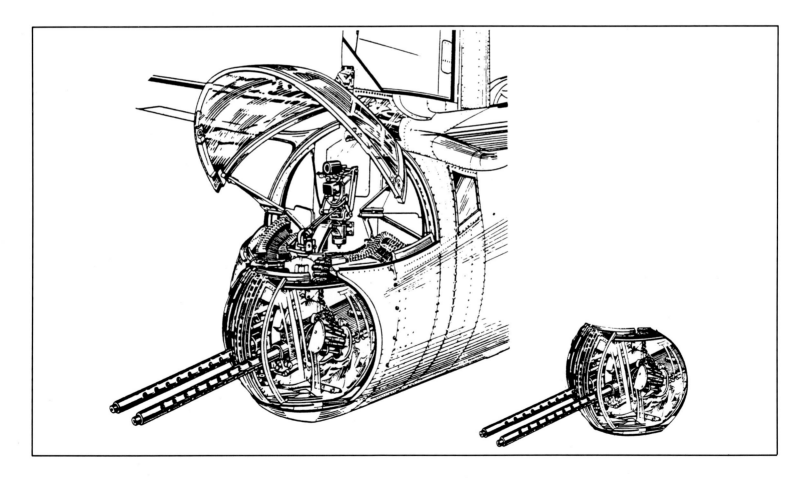

Promising tests were made with Bell power boost twin .50cal gun mounts set into modified greenhouse B-24D noses. The Bell unit adapted for this use was designed as a tail gun emplacement on the Martin B-26 Marauder, as depicted. Problems of supply, and the anticipated introduction of the B-24N, thwarted this modification.

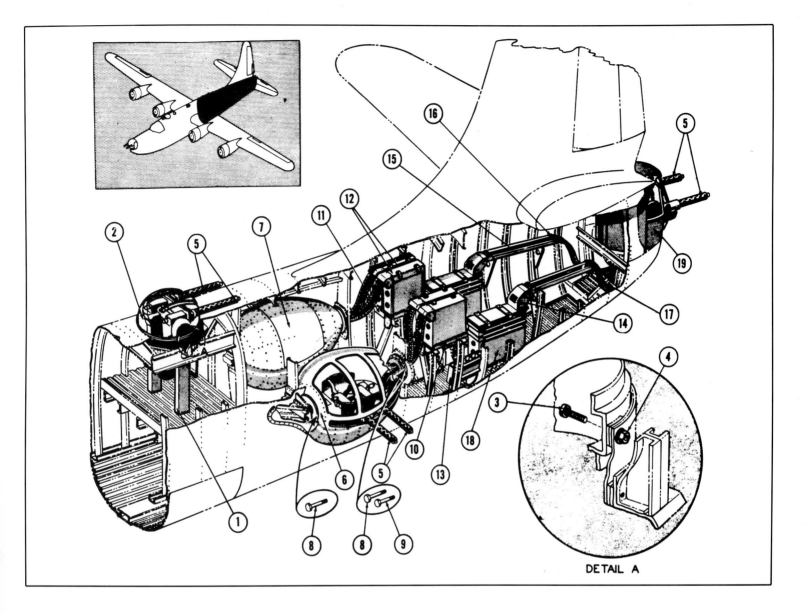

DETAIL A

ducting, according to the *Aviation* design analysis, was covered with sheet asbestos.

Consolidated's honeymoon with the Davis wing did not signify a break with traditional NACA thinking. The airfoil section of the B-24's vertical fin-and-rudder set used NACA 0007 cross section; the horizontal tail surface cross section was NACA 0015. The elevators of the B-24 had 30deg of up travel, and 20deg of down travel; the twin rudders had 10deg of movement either side of center.

### And a Box to Put It In

The fuselage of the B-24 was designed as a semi-monocoque shell reinforced with Z-section stringers, and transverse beltframes and bulkheads.

Beltframes were generally 18in apart. The longitudinal Z-stringers were typically spaced about 6in apart, but were grouped closer where needed for more strength. Longerons were used only to carry loads around openings like the bomb bays and access doors, or other places where the strength of the skin-and-stringer construction was interrupted. Convair designer J. H. Famme called the B-24's shape a four-sided modified eliptical fuselage.

### Liberator Roll Call

As B-24 development progressed, major and minor variants included the following:

*XB-24 (Air Corps serial number [s/n] 39-556):* First B-24; gross weight 41,000lb.

*Page from the Privateer Illustrated Parts Catalog reveal details of construction and interior furnishings. In the aft fuselage, micarta ammunition boxes mounted in pairs fed the twin .50cal machine guns of each ERCO blister turret. Other boxes fed the tail turret.*

*YB-24 (Air Corps s/ns 40-696–702 assigned, but all except 40-702 were delivered to the British as LB-30A):* Gross weight raised by 5,300lb above that of XB-24.

*B-24A (Air Corps s/ns 40-2369–2377):* First US production variant; .50cal guns replaced .30cal weapons; gross weight raised to 53,600lb.

15

*XB-24B (Air Corps s/n 39-680):* Renumbered prototype XB-24 with new engines using the characteristic oval cowlings of subsequent Liberators.

*B-24C (Air Corps s/ns 40-2378–2386):* Nine aircraft which might have been B-24Bs, but were called C-models with the addition of a Martin top turret and twin .50cal guns in the tail. The C-model was nearly three feet longer than earlier B-24s, and was similar in appearance to the first USAAF combat-ready B-24, the D-model.

*B-24D (AAF s/ns 40-2349–2368; 41-1087–1142; 41-11587–11938; 41-23640–24311; 41-24339; 42-40058–41257; 42-72765–72963; 42-63752–64046):* Number of this model built was 2,738 aircraft. D-models served in combat in Europe and the Pacific; need for increased frontal defensive firepower led to field and depot modifications with a B-24 tail turret mounted in the upper nose. Gross weight up to 60,000lb.

*B-24E (AAF s/ns 41-28409–28573; 41-29007–29008; 42-6976–7464; 42-7770; 41-29009–29115; 41-64395–64431):* Visually similar to B-24D; used different propeller; most were built under contract by Ford Motor Co. at Willow Run, Michigan. Knock-down kits of Ford E-models also were assembled by Douglas Aircraft Co. at Tulsa, Oklahoma, and Consolidated Aircraft Co. at Fort Worth, Texas.

*XB-24F (AAF s/n 41-11678):* Converted from a B-24D, retaining its original s/n; tested hot-air deicing system.

*B-24G (AAF s/ns 42-78045–78474):* Built by North American Aviation Incorporated in Dallas, Texas. After first 25 with D-style greenhouse, the G-models introduced Emerson nose turrets following the style already introduced on Ford B-24H models.

*B-24H (AAF s/ns 41-28574–29006; 42-51077–51225; 41-29116–29608; 42-50277–50451; 42-64432–64501; 42-*

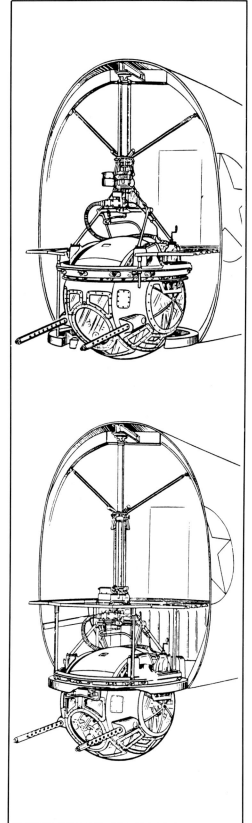

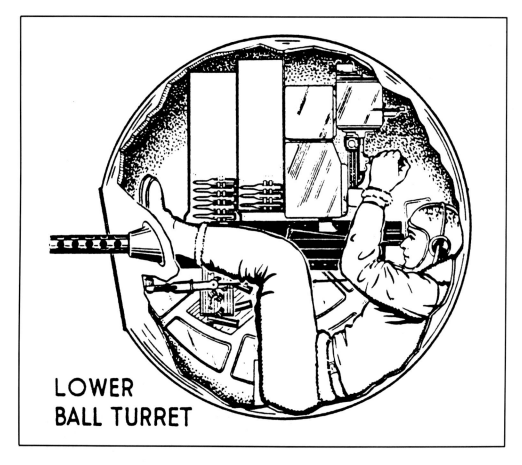

LOWER BALL TURRET

*Cutaway drawing from a World War II armaments catalog shows ball turret gunner in place, with internal ammo cans in his turret.*

*The B-24's ball turret shown in the retracted and extended positions.*

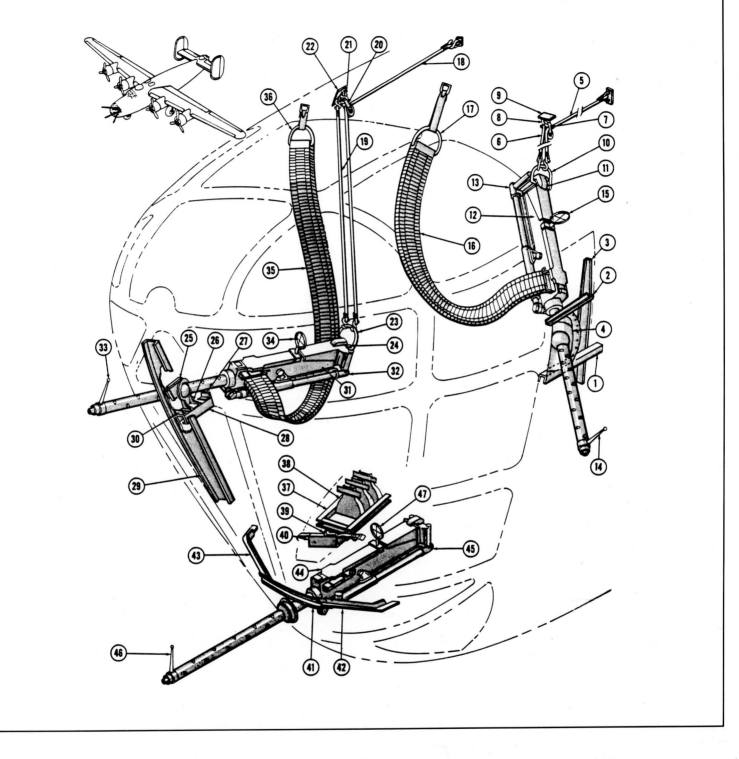

Greenhouse B-24s like the benchmark D-model were typically fitted with three .50cal nose machine guns in K-4 sockets, one in the lower nose, and one in each cheek. These used E-11-type recoil adaptors and C-19 mounts to attach the weapons to the sockets. Flexible feed chutes gave the guns more staying power than did small ammo cans that were quickly expended, sometimes requiring a one-sided lull in the middle of a gun-battle as the B-24 gunner swapped cans. In the greenhouse nose, the long, triangular bombsight window was made of laminated safety glass, much like car windows of the vintage.

Early British Liberator with short nose and gleaming natural aluminum propellers. Six British LB-30As were short-nose YB-24s placed in the hands of the British; twenty similar Liberator I models were known at Consolidated as LB-30Bs. Peter M. Bowers Collection

The pug-nose B-24A carried large flags proclaiming America's neutrality before the entry of the United States into World War II. The AAF's B-24As pioneered long-range air routes during the uneasy period prior to American participation in the conflict. The neutrality markings and insignia are painted over British-style camouflage. US Air Force via Jeff Ethell Collection

7465–7769; 42-52077–52776; 42-94729–95503): Built by Douglas, Convair Fort Worth, and Ford. *B-24I:* Not assigned.

*B-24J (AAF s/ns 42-50452–50508; 42-64047–64394; 42-99736–99935; 44-10253–10752; 44-44049–44501; 42-50509–51076; 42-51431–52076; 42-95504–95628; 44-48754–49001; 42-51226–51430; 42-72964–73514; 42-99936–100435; 42-109789–110188; 44-40049–41389; 42-78475–78794; 44-28061–28276):* Considered the definitive nose-turret B-24; gross weight was up to 65,000lb, from the XB-24's gross weight of only 41,000lb, for an increase of 12 tons over the prototype!

*XB-24K (AAF s/n 42-40234; modified from B-24D):* First AAF B-24 with a single tail; fitted with nose turret and updated equipment. Improved performance would lead to order for refined variant as B-24N. (Since Ford built the N-models, some confusion surrounds the sole K-model, which historian Allan Blue says was actually a Consolidated project at San Diego.)

*B-24L (AAF s/ns 44-41390–41806; 44-49002–50251):* Featured lightweight tail gun installation; the Eighth and Fifteenth Air Forces had difficulty standardizing on combat-capable features needed in B-24s, and hoped to iron out differences in L-model.

*B-24M (AAF s/ns 44-41807–42722; 44-50252–51928):* Last regular production B-24 model; late B-24Ms introduced a knife-edge canopy design.

*XB-24N (AAF s/n 44-48753) and YB-24N (AAF s/ns 44-52053–52059):* Single-tail Liberator with new nose and tail turrets, incorporating weight savings and more useful nose compartment for bombardier, navigator, and gunner. Improved performance over earlier models. Order of 5,168 production B-24Ns was canceled when European war ended.

*B-24O:* Not assigned.

*XB-24P:* Testbed made from B-24D s/n 42-40344.

*XB-24Q (AAF s/n 44-49916):* Converted B-24L used as test bed by General Electric Corp. (GE) for radar-directed B-47 tail turret.

*C-87 (AAF s/ns 42-107249–107275; 43-30548–36027 [including 3 C-87A models with 10 berths]; 44-*

*The last B-24A built for the AAF (40-2377) in latter-day garb, with late-1943-style national insignia and natural-metal finish not typically seen until 1944. Peter M. Bowers Collection*

*39198–39298; 44-52978–52987 [other C-87s and C-87As were included in B-24D s/n sequences]):* The C-87 was a remarkable production adaptation of the Liberator bomber into a viable transport, used around the world during the war. Typically, about 20 passengers and a crew of five could be carried in a C-87. More than 280 C-87s were built.

*C-109 (converted from B-24s):* Carried gasoline in special fuselage tanks, which could be pumped into ground storage tanks for later use. B-24 found favor for this task due to great range. Its huge tankage of volatile gasoline lent the nickname *C-One-Oh-Boom*, which may be largely undeserved.

*AT-22 (five converted C-87s):* Flying classrooms for flight-engineer training; later redesignated TB-24.

British Liberator II (LB-30) introduced the lengthened nose typical of subsequent B-24s (2ft, 7in longer than previous models), plus a slightly deeper aft fuselage that faired the horizontal stabilizer differently than on earlier Liberators. The 139 Liberator II/LB-30 bombers were the only Liberator series fitted with Curtiss Electric propellers instead of Hamilton Standard Hydramatics. Long prop domes of Curtiss Electric are visible on this 1941 view of Liberator II number AL543. Peter M. Bowers Collection

*F-7 (photo reconnaissance variant converted from B-24Hs):* F-7A and B were converted from B-24Js; carried cameras in bomb bay, or nose; saw service in the Pacific.

*XB-41 (AAF s/n 41-11822):* Converted from a B-24D, and intended as a large "escort fighter" for B-24 formations. Featured Bendix chin turret, two dorsal turrets (one elevated), and double waist guns. Developed in parallel

with XB-40 B-17 variant; XB-41 did not see combat or production status.

The US Navy desired Liberators for patrol missions. In a give-and-take trade, the Navy released its hold on Boeing Aircraft Co. assembly lines at Renton, Washington, in trade for a part of the San Diego Liberator production run, and the antisubmarine mission previously held by the USAAF. The first Navy Liberators, designated PB4Y-1, were similar to B-24Ds. Later PB4Y-1s were built with a round Engineering and Research Corp. (ERCO) bow turret, following some of the greenhouse versions that the Navy modified with the ERCO turret.

Though working independently of USAAF studies, the Navy also realized a single fin and rudder could enhance Liberator performance. The Navy answer was the PB4Y-2 Privateer, with a tail taller than the XB-24K, and a fuselage lengthened by more than seven feet. Naval designations for C-87 variants were RY-1 and RY-2; cargo version of the Privateer was RY-3, which

almost went into production for the AAF, as well as the C-87C. US Navy s/ns for Liberators and Privateers were as follows:

*PB4Y-1 (Navy Bureau of Aeronautics numbers [BuNo.] 31936–32287; 32288–32335; 38733–38979; 46725–46737; 63915–63959; 65287–65396; 90132–90271; 90462–90483):* Twin-tail Navy Liberator patrol bombers.

*XPB4Y-2 (BuNo. 32086; 32095–32096):* Prototypes converted from B-24Ds.

*PB4Y-2 (BuNo. 59350–60009; 66245–66324):* Gross weight 65,000lb; two top turrets, twin-gun power ERCO waist blisters; some carried Bat glide bombs on underwing stations.

*RY-1 (BuNo. 67797–67799).*

*RY-2 (BuNo. 39013–39017).*

*RY-3 (BuNo. 90020–90021; 90023–90059):* Single-tail transport variant similar to Privateer.

Navy Liberators and Privateers survived in postwar service longer than USAAF versions. PB4Y-1Ps were used

for photography. By 1951, the few Dash 1s still in service were redesignated P4Y-1P, along with Privateer P4Y-2, P4Y-2B (Bat bomb carriers), P4Y-2S antisubmarine patrollers, and P4Y-2K target drones. The Privateer even entered the new military unified nomenclature of 1962 when the remaining Privateer drones in Navy service received the basic designation P-4; their drone status and model letter designated them QP-4B.

The British used many Liberator models, including some RY-3 single-tail transports. Early short-nose Liberator I models were followed by Liberator IIs and LB-30s. LB-30 was a Consolidated designation for a land bomber, originally being produced for France, but diverted to England when France fell. Consolidated used the designation LB-30A to signify the six YB-24s transferred to the British, and LB-30B to denote the similar Liberator I. When the

*This classic Consolidated B-24D publicity photo still had the aircraft's tail number censored. This D-model was fitted with deicer boots covering nearly all the exposed edges of the vertical stabilizers.*

United States entered the war in December 1941, a number of LB-30s (British Liberator IIs with longer noses than previous variants) were taken

21

*The first Liberator assembled at Consolidated's Fort Worth, Texas, factory was D-model 41-11705, made of subassemblies shipped from the San Diego, California, Consolidated plant.*

over by the USAAF. These were hybrid Liberators, employing an aft location for the top turret which was a four-gun (.303cal) Boulton-Paul turret on British LB-30s, and a Martin two-gun .50cal turret on the American LB-30s.

LB-30s saw combat in the 7th Bombardment Group in the Pacific in 1942. USAAF LB-30s also bombed in the Aleutians and patrolled the Panama Canal Zone. When not serving as bombers, some LB-30s were set up for regular transport runs in the Pacific, ultimately receiving many C-87–style modifications. Some of these converted bombers outlived the war to become civil transports and freight haulers.

*Line-up of Liberators at Fort Worth includes desert-sand examples in three positions nearest camera, followed by two early Navy PB4Y-1s, another AAF B-24D, and some bombers with mismatched olive-drab and desert-sand vertical tail components. Second row of planes in upper right of photo includes C-87 Liberator Express transports.* Ivan Stepnich Collection

*A red-cowled B-24D being marshaled on the ramp for parking.* US Air Force via Jeff Ethell Collection

Wash's Tub, *a well-aecorated early D-model, returned to the States after combat, eventually being scrapped at Spokane, Washington.* US Air Force

US Navy RY-1 was a C-87A equivalent, with 10 sleeper berths and R-1830-45 engines instead of the -43s of straight C-87s. Peter M. Bowers Collection

North American-built B-24Gs at the factory flightline near Dallas, Texas, show details of fuselage bulkhead immediately behind nose turret. Irregularly scalloped gray paint on undersides of fuselage and engine nacelles is different from Consolidated's straight feathered demarcation. North American Aviation

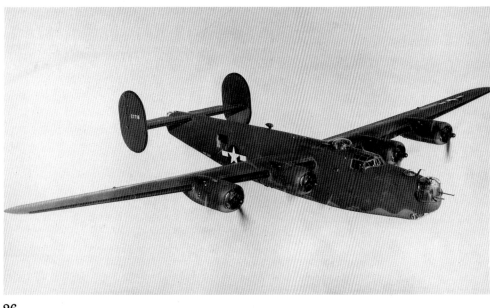

The North American B-24G, although the lowest-letter B-24 with a factory nose turret, actually received nose turret later in its production life than did the B-24H. Waves in camouflage demarcation on this North American example tends to be less regular than those used on Ford-built B-24s. North American Aviation

Ford B-24H (42-7718) shows scalloped fuselage paint, with straight nacelle demarcation curving up to wing juncture. This plane is fitted with enclosed waist window mounts. Peter M. Bowers Collection

*Natural-metal B-24J-145-CO on the ramp at San Diego shows old-style disappearing nosewheel doors and MPC nose turret. The antiglare panel stops mid-astrodome.* Convair

*This view of a B-24J from Fort Worth highlights the high-aspect-ratio Davis wing. The anti-glare panel extends all the way to nose turret.* Peter M. Bowers Collection

*The sole XB-24K was a Consolidated San Diego single-tail test bed using components from a Douglas B-23 vertical tail and, later, a C-54 horizontal tail. Originally, the conversion was performed on B-24D 42-40058. Later 1943, the single-tail aft fuselage was removed and grafted on a vastly updated B-24D, featuring a nose turret and other new components, and carrying number 42-40234, generally acknowledged as the definitive XB-24K.*

*B-24M-31-FO shows late-production features—knife-edge windscreen, hooded turbo-superchargers, and large, rectangular navigator windows.* Peter M. Bowers Collection

*XB-24N was a harbinger of sporty single-tail Liberators that never got into large-scale production by war's end. Armament updates replaced traditional nose and tail turrets with new gun emplacements. R-1830-75 engines were used.* Peter M. Bowers Collection

*Navy RY-3 shows openable waist window on right side of fuselage; on left side, cargo doors took up this area.* Liberator Club

*Chapter 2*

# Calendar of Combat

Information from the official US Air Force *Combat Chronology: 1941–1945,* compiled by Kit C. Carter and Robert Mueller, illuminates the Liberator's war. The following details characterize AAF B-24 operations. Virtually daily, somewhere in the world, between Pearl Harbor Day and VJ-Day, Liberators plied their craft. The following highlights are just that—highlights. Additional B-24 operations took place; those excerpted here provide an overview of the Liberator at war. AAF B-24s were a huge part of the overall air armada that contributed to the downfall of the Axis around the world. As the B-24s carried the war to the enemy, so did many other warplanes, sometimes in concert with the Liberators. The Air Force log frequently attributes aircraft to their numbered air force, rather than individual bomb groups or squadrons. The chronology often accommodates the mixed B-24 and B-17 operations (especially of the Eighth Air Force) by merely referencing HBs—heavy bombers—for a day's missions, inadvertently obscuring what

*Armorers fuzed 100lb practice bombs beside a 466th BG B-24 of the Eighth AF in England.* Jeff Ethell Collection

role the ever-present B-24s played in that bomber force. Herewith is a diary of the war of the B-24s:

The first American Liberator combat loss was a ground casualty at Hickam Field on December 7, 1941. It was a B-24A, s/n 40-2371.

In early 1942, LB-30s carried the war to the Japanese as Fifth Air Force (AF) crews tried in vain to thwart a Japanese convoy approaching Java on February 27. Bombing results were not a significant factor in the Battle of Java Sea, and by March 1, the American heavy bombers flew their last mission from Java. The next day, three of the LB-30s joined five B-17s in evacuating the last 260 soldiers from Jogjakarta—the last airstrip on Java still under Allied control. Japanese troops were about 20mi away as the LB-30s roared off the runway.

On June 4, 1942, a B-24 was missing after Eleventh AF attacks on a Japanese carrier force in the Aleutians. The Japanese presence in these Alaskan islands was timed to coincide with the enemy's attack on Midway. The following day, two Eleventh AF LB-30s joined other bombers and fighters in a search for the Japanese fleet that did not find the ships. On the night of June 6–7, General Tinker, commander of the Seventh AF, led a flight of LB-30s from Midway to bomb Wake. The Liberator carrying Tinker appeared to stall and crash at sea. On June 8, a lone LB-30 flying armed patrol found Japanese naval units in Kiska Harbor in the Aleutians. By June 11, the Air Force chronology listed five B-24s in the Eleventh AF arsenal being dispatched to bomb Japanese targets at Kiska, along with an equal number of B-17s. The bombers made low-level attacks on two cruisers and a destroyer; antiaircraft fire downed one of the B-24s. The other four Liberators were chased by four Japanese fighters back to Umnak, until American fighters drove the enemy away. The next day, one of the B-24s in Alaska joined six B-17s in a return engagement over Kiska Harbor that left one Japanese cruiser damaged and a destroyer burning.

Halfway around the world, spanning the night of June 11–12, 1942, 13 B-24Ds of the HALPRO (for Halverson Project) Detachment under Col. Harry A. Halverson rose from Fayid, Egypt, to drop bombs in the first attack on the Romanian oil fields of Ploesti. A dozen of Halverson's Liberators made the bomb run at dawn. The Liberators recovered at scattered locations in Iraq, Syria, and Turkey, the latter country impounding the four B-24s that entered Turkish airspace. Damage to Ploesti was light, but the tone was set

31

*Jerk's Natural was a 93rd BG B-24D that spent considerable time away from England in North Africa, where RAF-style fin flashes were used. The black ring around the star probably was used to dull a yellow ring applied to Allied aircraft during the earlier Operation Torch in North Africa. The star was dulled with gray paint to diminish its visibility at a distance. Medium green blotching was applied to some olive-drab B-24s to break up their lines. The survival of original World War II color photography is due almost exclusively to durable Kodachrome films of that era. US Air Force via Jeff Ethell Collection*

for future combat by Americans in Liberators in the Middle East. Three days later, seven HALPRO B-24Ds were joined by a pair of British Royal Air Force (RAF) Liberators, and torpedo-laden RAF Beaufort twin-engine bombers as they attacked the Italian Navy east of Malta. The B-24s claimed damage to a battleship and a cruiser.

That same day, two Eleventh AF B-24s and three B-17s were forced to abort their intended bombing of Kiska because of weather. (The AAF record for the Aleutians reveals the worst possible weather for sustained flying operations. Weather aborts, and aircraft lost in weather, abounded in this far-northern battlefield. The Liberator crews—and their compatriots in the Eleventh AF—gallantly fought a little-

known war, and deserve recognition for their pluck in the face of cold, ice, fog, snow, rain, and wind during most of the year.)

On June 18, 1942, one LB-30 and four B-24s made up the Liberator component of an eight-ship heavy bomber force that struck Kiska Harbor from high altitude. As the Liberators and Fortresses left Kiska, they tallied one enemy transport ship blazing and sinking, with another damaged. One of the B-24s crashed in the water; some of its crew members were rescued.

Nine of the HALPRO B-24Ds arrived over Bengasi Harbor, Libya, at night on June 21 after RAF Wellington bombers illuminated the target area with flares and incendiaries. In North African operations in 1942 and 1943,

*Its 90th BG bomber days over, B-24D Pug Nose flew transport runs with its top turret deleted.* Lee Bushnell Collection

American and British airpower worked closely. AAF planes quickly adopted the RAF-style fin flash of red, white, and blue as an Allied recognition feature; on twin-tail aircraft including Liberators, the flash appeared on the insides as well as the outsides.

Throughout June and July, Eleventh AF B-24s and LB-30s, often operating with B-17s, launched bombing missions against targets including Kiska. Weather pre-empted some sorties.

Seventh AF LB-30s staged through Midway the night of June 26–27, and bombed Wake Island. For the first half of the initial year of war for the United States, Liberator bombing missions were almost exclusively performed by small groups of planes in Alaska, North Africa, and the Central and South Pacific. The B-24 as mass strategic weapon was yet to be realized.

On the night of June 29–30, AAF B-24s bombed Libya's Tobruk Harbor. When one of the Liberators was lost, the first US combat casualties in the Middle East occurred.

The Fourth of July 1942 saw deadly pyrotechnics in the Mediterranean as B-24s attacked a convoy the night of July 4–5, flaming one tanker. More B-24s visited enemy shipping in Bengasi Harbor that night.

The build-up of American forces in North Africa and Alaska in 1942 prompted some late logistical switches. The 404th Bomb Squadron (BS), its B-24s already painted desert sand for North Africa, was dispatched to the Alaskan Theater instead, arriving on July 8. Crews called these Liberators Pink Elephants because of the hue of the desert-sand paint.

On July 9, 1942, six Liberators in the Mediterranean, on their way to

shipping targets, were jumped by enemy fighters. One B-24 was shot down, and the other five returned without bombing their objective. It was a lesson that would become clear in every theater: No matter how well gunned, B-24s (and B-17s) were vulnerable to fighter attacks.

On July 11, Japanese seaplane fighters attacked four B-24s taking off for a Kiska strike. These Liberators persisted without loss, and bombed a Japanese cruiser with unobserved results.

The HALPRO B-24s were redesignated the Halverson BS on July 17. Along with the 9th BS, which had 19

33

*Battle-scarred B-24D of the Liberandos cruises past Mount Vesuvius, Italy.*

B-24s and nine B-17s, these Liberators then formed the 1st Provisional Group on July 20, 1942, still under the command of Col. Harry Halverson at Lydda, Palestine. As the summer of 1942 unfolded, AAF Liberator combat operations continued primarily in the Middle East and Alaska. Harbor bombing—whether at Tobruk and Bengasi, or Kiska—saw B-24s and an occasional Alaskan LB-30 being employed to support the objectives of surface forces. On August 21, B-24s from two squadrons intercepted an enemy convoy southwest of Crete. Liberator crews claimed two ships probably sunk. Enemy fighters picked off a straggling B-24, which then ditched at sea. Liberator operations were launched almost daily in this period. The Alaska sorties continued to suffer a high number of aborts due to weather and mechanical problems.

On September 6, an Eleventh AF B-24 on armed reconnaissance patrol over Tanaga sank a Japanese mine layer and strafed a tender, as well as tents and buildings on shore. The majestic heavy bomber could pinch-hit on the deck, too.

During the nights of September 16–17 and 19–20, B-24s ranged to Greece to attack shipping in this German-held country. Late in September, the 90th Bomb Group (BG), a pioneer of Pacific B-24 operations, paused in Hawaii to fill a void in the force of heavy bombers deemed necessary for the protection of the islands.

On September 25, the Eleventh AF put up nine B-24s for bombing and a tenth for photography as part of a formation including B-17s and P-39 and P-40 escorts. This marked the Eleventh's first combined American-Canadian mission as Royal Canadian Air Force (RCAF) Kittyhawks joined the armada. The number of B-24s in Alaska grew during 1942 to afford the Eleventh AF the opportunity to launch a total of 14 B-24s plus one LB-30 recon plane on September 27. Though small by later European Theater of Operations (ETO) air-war standards, this force represented gathering momentum in Alaska. The next day, a B-24

and an LB-30 bombed installations on Attu. Over Bengasi on October 6, two B-24s went down as heavy, accurate flak, and fighters, challenged the Liberators.

Because the Eighth AF ultimately operated vast fleets of B-24s and B-17s, many notations in the Air Force combat chronology only list the number of heavy bombers dispatched, without calling out specific types. The first notation for the Eighth specifically citing use of B-24s was on October 9, 1942, when Liberators participated in the first American mission in which more than 100 bombers were sent from England to bomb the Continent. Five targets in France were hit by the combined forces.

The Tenth AF used B-24s on October 21, 1942, for the first heavy bomber mission over China, and the first AAF bomb strike north of the Yangtze and Yellow Rivers. The Liberators were part of the India Air Task Force (IATF). They staged through Chengtu, China, and bombed coal mines at Linhsi. As conceived, the mission was to bomb nearby power stations and pumps in order to flood the mines, denying their output to the Japanese. The bombing did not succeed in flooding the coal mines, but did damage the target area. As described in the Strategic Bombing Survey for the Pacific war, Japan was resource-poor, and dependent upon its conquered territory for materials, including coal, to drive its wartime economy. Hence, an ongoing emphasis on interrupting the flow of raw materials to Japan had deliberate consequences on Japan's war-making capability.

United States Army, Middle East Air Forces (USAMEAF) activated the Liberator-equipped 376th BG at Lydda, Palestine, on October 31, 1942. The 376th replaced the 1st Provisional Group, and was placed under the original group's commander, Col. George F. McGuire. At first, the 376th was envisioned as part of an English-American air force that would be dispatched to the Caucasus to help the Soviet Union. But that idea was not realized, and the 376th stayed in the Middle East. On November 7, the 376th began the move from Palestine to Egypt.

Two days later, Gen. Carl Spaatz acknowledged to Gen. Dwight D.

Eisenhower that any more air force build-ups in North Africa must of necessity erode build-ups in England, because no other theaters had force levels considered reducible. That same day, the Eighth AF launched an experimental attack by B-24s and B-17s from reduced altitudes on the submarine base at Saint-Nazaire, in occupied France. Twelve Liberators, bombing from 17,500–18,300ft, sustained but little flak damage, while 31 B-17s flying at 7,500–10,000ft suffered three shootdowns and 22 planes damaged. Low-level heavy bomber attacks on German submarine bases were not pursued after this. (Ultimately, the U-boat threat would be neutralized on the high seas, often by Liberators.)

On November 12, 1942, the US-AMEAF was dissolved and replaced by the Ninth AF. The next day, the 98th BG arrived in Egypt from Palestine, to bolster Ninth AF Liberator assets, as Tobruk fell to the British Eighth Army. In the hard-fighting Fifth AF, on November 17, 1942, a lone B-24 bombed the Japanese-held Rabaul wharf area as Liberators added their might to the fight for the South Pacific.

On November 20, IATF B-24s of the Tenth AF bombed the Mandalay marshaling yards as these B-24s stepped up their campaign against Japanese targets in Thailand and Burma. By November 23, 1942, Eighth AF crews reported a noticeable shift in enemy fighter tactics as the fighters perceived the B-24s' and B-17s' relatively weak defenses against frontal attacks. The fighters began more head-on attacks instead of attacks from the rear.

*The 93rd BG fielded olive-drab B-24Ds in European combat, as this 1943 photo depicts.* US Air Force via Jeff Ethell Collection

(Ultimately, this would precipitate an ongoing struggle to add power nose turrets to B-24s and B-17s, as well as heavy cockpit armor, especially in the Eighth AF, where Liberators and Fortresses were often fitted with thick slabs of armor glass in the cockpit. Some Eighth B-24s clearly showed the application of external bolt-on armor plating on the fuselage beside the cockpit area.)

On December 4, 1942, the Ninth AF sent B-24s in the first attack by American bombers on Italy. The Italian fleet and docks at Naples reeled from

*Overcast on November 24, 1944, did not stop this Eighth AF B-24 from releasing a stick of 12 bombs over Europe.* US Air Force

the bomb tonnage. Hits were claimed on a battleship, among three or four ships struck, as well as harbor targets and a railyard. The next day, Fifth AF B-24s bombed the Japanese airfield at Kavieng on New Ireland, northeast of New Guinea.

A year after the Japanese attack on Pearl Harbor, three squadrons of B-24s from the 93rd BG arrived in North Africa from England to add to the Twelfth AF inventory.

On December 8, 1942, B-17s and a lone B-24 of the Fifth AF attacked six Japanese destroyers bringing troops to reinforce the Buna-Gona beachhead, which was then under Allied ground assault. The six destroyers were discouraged by the heavy bombers and turned back for the Japanese stronghold at Rabaul. It was a textbook example of how prewar planners thought heavy bombers would be employed; in actual combat, such routs of warships were infrequent. (Five days later, B-17s and B-24s intercepted a convoy of five Japanese destroyers again steaming for Buna with reinforcements; this time, the heavy bombers did not deter the enemy convoy.)

By December 12, the Ninth AF's Bomber Command exercised operational control over RAF Liberators as they attacked the Naples dock area. The operational control of these RAF Liberators would be common through the end of 1942. On December 14, the Eighth AF's inspector general reported that the diversion of Eighth AF assets to equip the Twelfth AF in North Africa (as with the B-24s of the 93rd BG) was seriously hindering Eighth training and combat programs.

On December 21, single-ship Fifth AF B-24 strikes against Japanese shipping and barges north of Finschhafen, New Guinea, and in the mouth of the Mambare River, as well as near Cape Ward Hunt, reflected local doctrine that led to the use of Liberators individually in the Pacific far more than over European targets.

December 22 was a harbinger of a dreary future for Japanese forces when the Seventh AF launched a remarkable 26 B-24s against Wake Island, bombing the night of December 22–23 after staging through Midway, from Hawaii. A dozen Tenth AF B-24s bombed docks, a railway station, an arsenal, and a powerplant at Bangkok on December 26. Three days later, the same-size B-24 formation from IATF attacked shipping around Rangoon, in southern Burma.

On the last day of 1942, Ninth AF B-24s and RAF Liberators bombed docks and shipping at Sfax, Tunisia, with good effect. That same day, in the South Pacific, Fifth AF B-24s, operating singly, bombed the Japanese-held airfield at Gasmata, New Britain, and attacked shipping in Wide Bay and Saint George Channel. Meanwhile, six Eleventh AF B-24s, protected by an escort of nine P-38s, attacked Kiska Harbor, hitting two cargo vessels. Six Japanese fighters intercepted the B-24s and P-38s; one enemy plane was listed as a probable kill. The first full year of war for the AAF drew to a close with Liberators on several fronts.

The best plans of the AAF could be undone by weather. On January 2, 1943, the Eighth AF sent four radar-equipped B-24s on a "moling" intruder mission to harass the Germans. The idea was to use cloud cover that made mass bombing unfeasible (in the days before advanced radar-bombing and radio-bombing techniques), by having the moling B-24s alert enemy air-raid crews north of the Ruhr Valley, in northwestern Germany, thus causing an expenditure of German activity to meet a nonexistent threat above the clouds. However, this mission and two more attempts in January were thwarted when clear weather over the

target area allowed the Germans to see that there was no serious bomber formation.

In the Pacific, the takeover of Buna Mission on January 2 by Australian and American forces exemplified what would follow: repeated air strikes, many by B-24s, to prepare a site for ultimate land invasion.

On January 5, the Ninth AF sent the 93rd BG's B-24s against Sousse Harbor, Tunisia, when the primary target—Tunis—was obscured by clouds. That night, RAF Liberators from 160 Squadron, under Ninth AF operational control, revisited both harbors. On January 16, the Ninth AF B-24s bombed Tripoli Harbor and town, and RAF Liberators from 178 Squadron struck at Tripoli's Benito Gate and a road junction.

On January 20, Tenth AF B-24s, on the largest mission in the theater to date, flew reconnaissance that revealed new railway construction by the Japanese between Thailand and Burma. The Tenth AF gained more Liberator crews when the 492nd BS, new to combat, borrowed four B-24s and one crew from the 436th BS, with which to mount a nine-plane strike against Rangoon docks.

As January 1943 closed, the Seventh AF applied increased pressure in the Central Pacific. After six B-24s dropped 60 bombs on Wake on January 25, the Seventh sent out three Liberators the next day from Funafuti in the Ellice Islands to fly photo reconnaissance over Tarawa, Maiana, Abemama, Beru, and Tomama, in the Gilbert Islands. Over the lagoon at Tarawa, the B-24s attacked a merchant ship.

By February 8, the Tenth AF was able to put up 18 B-24s to hit Rangoon rail facilities. On February 12, the unit loaded seven B-24s with the first 2,000lb blockbusters used in the China-Burma-India (CBI) Theater of Operations. The blockbusters failed to damage the Myitnge Bridge. A dozen other Tenth B-24s returned to Rangoon the same day.

The Thirteenth AF's 424th BS, part of the 307th BG, first sent its B-24s into combat February 13, 1943, in an attack on Buin and on shipping in the Shortland Islands that turned deadly when Japanese fighters ripped into the Liberators' light fighter cover,

destroying half of the B-24s and three escorting fighters. The next day, nine B-24s with light fighter protection again attacked Buin. Again, stiff Japanese fighter opposition downed two B-24s. The cumulative loss of five Thirteenth AF B-24s in two days prompted a halt in all their daylight bombing missions until adequate fighter escort could be provided.

Tenth AF B-24s pressured the Japanese on the night of February 22–23 when 10 Liberators mined a section of the Gulf of Martaban in southern Burma. A force of 24 B-24s and RAF Liberators flew a diversionary strike against Rangoon and Mingaladon airfield.

On March 2, the Fifth AF regimen of single-plane B-24 strikes was altered for the Battle of Bismarck Sea. B-17s and B-24s attacked a 16-ship Japanese convoy comprised of equal numbers of transports and destroyers steaming from Rabaul toward Huon Gulf. First bombed north of New Britain, the convoy was last bombed that day between New Guinea and New Britain. By day's end, half the transports were sunk or sinking, according to AAF reports. The next day, the heavy bombers were joined by other American and Australian planes and US Navy PT boats. By the end of day two, all eight transports had been sunk and airpower had demolished half the destroyers, as well as a large part of the Japanese fighter planes covering the convoy. On March 4, Allied planes continued bombing remnants of the convoy in Huon Gulf, thereby closing the Battle of Bismarck Sea as a decisive defeat for the Japanese. This marked the last try by the Japanese to use large ships to reinforce positions on Huon Gulf. Though not strictly a B-24 action, Liberators took part.

On March 6, the Eighth AF launched 15 B-24s on a diversionary attack on a bridge and U-boat facilities at Brest, France, while a main force of heavy bombers attacked a power plant and other targets at Lorient. (When Germany proper was bombed, American planners discounted the value of bombing German power plants because of the largely erroneous assumption that Germans could shunt power over redundant systems to restore electrical energy to any section of the country af-

*Picturesque mosaic of European farm fields underlays smoky ribbons from marker flares dropped by an Eighth AF B-24.* Kiernan Collection

fected. In reality, German officials expressed concern that the Allies would destroy an electrical system that often had insufficient redundancy.)

B-24s bombed Rabaul on March 11. The AAF in the Pacific, including the available and growing number of B-24s, attacked the problem of strategic targets differently than did their European counterparts. The tenuous reach of Japanese supply lines made attacks on shipping and individual bases take on a greater strategic significance than that in Europe.

On March 15, Liberators of Fifth AF units and Australian warplanes attacked targets on Dobo, in the Arol Islands, and Wokam. Joint US-Australian operations would continue, sometimes involving Liberators operated by both countries' air forces.

During this period, Tenth AF B-24s repeatedly bombed bridges and viaducts in the CBI; Fifth AF Liberators went after shipping and airfields, and Ninth AF B-24s revisited Naples and other targets useful to the impending Allied invasion of Sicily and Italy, including ferries and harbor installations at Palermo and Messina. The plucky Eleventh AF continued to launch against targets including Kiska.

Indicative of the build-up of B-24s, the Eleventh AF was able to muster 16 B-24s on April Fool's Day 1943, against Kiska. The large (for Alaska) group of Liberators joined B-25s and P-38s in attacking ships, camps, and the beach area. The next day, 18 more B-24s launched sorties against Kiska, while four Liberators bombed the runway on Attu. (The previous day, preparations were ordered for Operation Landgrab—the Allied invasion of Attu.) By April 15, the Eleventh mustered 23 B-24s, launching from Adak to strike Kiska.

The Thirteenth AF sent three B-24s on harassing strikes against Kahili airfield in Bougainville in the Solomon Islands on April 10. Just as the Japanese sent single-ship night bombers over American airfields, the AAF sent B-24s, often at night, and often alone and spread several hours after the previous solo B-24, to bomb Japanese airfields. Reasons were many: The harassing strikes deprived enemy personnel of rest; they cratered runways, to temporarily slow operations and necessitate expenditure of manpower; they destroyed aircraft and enemy equipment; and they forced the Japanese to commit some resources to antiaircraft protection.

On April 11, a Ninth AF B-24 went down on a mission over Naples Harbor. Intense flak and fighting took a toll of the formation, while the B-24's gunners claimed three enemy fighters downed.

Factories formerly used by Ford and General Motors Corp. in Antwerp, Belgium, were the target of 65 Eighth AF heavy bombers on May 4. A mixed group of 34 B-17s and B-24s were successful in their feint toward the French coastline, drawing more than 100 German fighters—more than half the enemy fighters in the area—aloft. Many of these fighters drawn away from the main bomber force were unable to interfere with its mission.

As American forces were establishing their landing on Attu in the Aleutians, the Eleventh AF sent a single B-24 on May 11 for use as an air-to-ground liaison plane, while B-24 supply-dropping sorties were flown in support of the troops. Poor weather obscured some B-24 bombardment missions, and one B-24 dropped leaflets over Attu. A May 15 mission to bomb Wake by Seventh AF B-24s from Midway netted mixed results: seven B-24s bombed Wake, four aborted, and seven others failed to find the target. Twenty-two Japanese fighters attacked the bombers. One B-24 was lost, and B-24 gunners claimed four Japanese planes shot down.

On June 4, six Eleventh AF B-24s followed a Navy Ventura bomber and made a radar-bombing run over North Head, in the Aleutians. The Eleventh continued to use other B-24s as air-to-ground liaison aircraft in the theater.

When the US War Department diverted the 389th BG from England to North Africa on June 7, the Eighth AF lost another building block in its strategic plan. The 389th subsequently was to play a role in the famous August low-level mission against Ploesti's oil refineries in August.

On June 26, the 93rd BG's Liberators left England for North Africa, in anticipation of heavy bombardment requirements for the invasion of Sicily and the low-level Ploesti oil refinery raid. The next day, the Eighth AF's 44th BG took its B-24s to North Africa as well, as the 201st Bomb Wing (Provisional) was attached to the Ninth AF in the Mediterranean, for operations between July 2 and August 21.

Seventh AF Liberators continued long-range missions in the Central Pacific. On June 28, 1943, a bombing mission by Seventh units dwindled from attrition. Of 19 B-24s launched from Hawaii, one crashed at an en route stage stop at Palmyra, to the south. Of the 18 Liberators reaching the forward staging base of Funafuti, two were released from the mission because of engine trouble. When two more of the B-24s crashed as the bombers were taking off from Funafuti, eight more B-24s were grounded following the second crash. This left a force of only six B-24s

aloft for the mission to bomb Nauru. Two of these aborted, and two more did not find Nauru because of a weather front. At last, only two B-24s of 19 dispatched from Hawaii actually bombed Nauru, with unobserved results.

On July 8, Fourteenth AF units put aloft 22 B-24s, escorted by 13 P-40s, to attack shipping, docks, and a cement works at Haiphong in French Indochina. Nine B-24s returned to Haiphong two days later, and three were in the vicinity again on July 11.

The Ninth AF, bolstered by B-24s sent down from England, launched about 80 Liberators to drop bombs on the marshaling yards at Naples on July 17. One B-24 was shot down, and several others received damage as a result of stiff fighter challenges. The B-24 gunners claimed 23 enemy fighters.

On July 18, 21 B-24s from Thirteenth AF units joined P-40s, P-38s, and about 140 Navy and Marine dive-bombers and fighters in a thorough attack on Japanese facilities at Kahili. Fifteen of the Liberators went after the Kahili airfield, bombing antiaircraft emplacements, runways, and revetments.

In the Mediterranean, the Ninth AF flexed its Liberator strength by launching more than 100 B-24s on July 19. They bombed railyards at Littoria, in central Italy, and a nearby airfield. On the flight home, railroads at Orlando and Anzio were bombed too. Effective Italian railroads—a success for

*A grateful 449th BG airman poses in the flak hole in the left wing of his B-24 in Italy after a nearly fatal mission. Chet Goad Collection*

Benito Mussolini's regime—were significant targets in the Italian bombing campaign. As the war in Italy progressed, everything from P-47 fighter-bombers to B-24s were employed to stop the trains from aiding the Axis war effort.

The climactic push against the Japanese base at Munda in the Solomons on July 25 involved the heaviest air attack to date in the South Pacific. Included in the American air armada were Thirteenth AF B-24s and some remaining Pacific B-17s. Later that day, 10 more B-24s, with escort, bombed Bibolo Hill. The ground assault on the area opened the same day.

The cadence of the war, prosecuted by determined Allies, delivered bases closer to the shrinking Japanese perimeter as the last half of 1943 unfolded. Signaling the acquisition of closer airfields was the Seventh AF's last mission against Wake to be launched from Midway, on July 26. During this strike, eight B-24s bombed an oil storage area. About 20 Japanese fighters attacked the Liberators; a possible sighting of a German FW 190 among the attackers most likely was in error. Rumored to be in Japanese service, and even given an Allied code

*The 718th BS of the 449th BG put B-24s over the Alps. Plane nearest camera has lightweight tail gun emplacement. Chet Goad Collection*

name, FW 190s do not appear to have actually been used by Japan, according to historian Rene Francillon.

Fighter pilots flying P-47 Thunderbolts handed the Luftwaffe a surprise on July 30, 1943, as the Americans escorted Eighth AF bombers when German fighters attacked over Bocholt. This was a deeper penetration than the Luftwaffe was accustomed to, and was made possible by the auxiliary gas tanks the P-47s carried. The advent of long-ranging escort fighters would enable B-24s and B-17s of Eighth AF units to carry the war deep into Germany.

On the last day of July 1943, AAF Liberator operations included a nine-plane mission by Tenth AF B-24s to lay mines in the Rangoon River.

August 1, 1943, was the fateful date of Operation Tidal Wave—the minimum-altitude strike by 177 Ninth AF B-24s against Romanian oil refineries at Ploesti. Noncombat attrition be-

gan over water on the long flight to Romania, and accelerated dramatically when the bombers came under fire over land. Ultimately, 54 Liberators and 532 aviators were lost on this mission, but significant damage was registered on the refineries, despite navigational mix-ups that saw some targets bombed by more B-24s than briefed, and others less heavily hit.

The increasing tempo of the American war effort was manifested in Alaska on August 4, when the Eleventh AF logged a one-day record of 153 tons of bombs dropped on Kiska. The mixed force of attacking planes included a total of 25 B-24 sorties in at least two groupings.

Pressure on the German war machine increased on August 13 when 61 B-24s launched the first Ninth AF raid on Austria, bombing an aircraft factory at Wiener-Neustadt. The Ninth returned the next day, intent on destroying Bf 109 fighters before they could be completed.

In Alaska, on August 13, 1943, an Eleventh AF B-24 flew a "special" reconnaissance mission, according to the official AAF history. The next day, it launched two B-24s on radar ferret and reconnaissance flights. Ferrets were

specially instrumented aircraft that probed enemy installations.

On August 15, American and Canadian troops invaded Kiska. An eerie silence greeted the Allies—the Japanese took advantage of the frequent Aleutian fogs to evacuate their garrison.

The Ninth AF sent 86 B-24s to bomb an area of the city, and airfields, at Foggia, Italy, on August 16.

The wandering 44th, 93rd, and 389th BGs brought their B-24s back to England from the Mediterranean in time to resume Eighth AF operations on September 8.

Ranging out from Canton Island in the central Pacific, Seventh AF B-24s on September 8 fired their machine guns at a Japanese flying boat, but no visible damage could be discerned.

The war in the Far East caused its share of attrition. On September 15, 1943, four of five B-24s attacking a Haiphong cement plant were shot down by an enemy fighter force estimated at 50 aircraft. The surviving B-24 claimed 10 enemy fighters downed by its gunners.

War in the Mediterranean demanded more heavy bombers, so Gen. Dwight Eisenhower requested that the Eighth AF send the veteran 44th, 93rd, and 389th BGs back. Their return to the Med occurred on September 16.

When American commanders wanted to prevent Japanese attacks on US installations at Baker Island and in the Ellice Islands by taking the Japanese at Tarawa out of the fight, 24 Seventh AF B-24s, rising from Funafuti and Canton Island, bombed multiple targets in the Gilbert Islands on the night of September 18–19, as part of a coordinated Army-Navy attack.

The Ninth AF launched its last mission from North Africa, on September 22. It was a B-24 strike on Maritsa and Eleusis airfields. The bomb groups of IX Bomber Command subsequently were assigned to the Twelfth AF in the Med. The Ninth AF emerged as a tactical air force in England, established on October 16. The Twelfth was willing to expand the B-24s' repertoire, and sent Liberators on a low-level raid to bomb Italian bridges on October 19.

On October 25, more than 60 Fifth AF B-24s bombed Rabaul, claiming about 20 airplanes destroyed on the ground. Between 60 and 70 Japanese fighters contested the Liberators' presence, and B-24 gunners claimed more than 30 shot down in a running gun battle. The volume of this day's Rabaul strike was a far cry from the small efforts mounted in the beginning of the year.

On November 1, 1943, the Fifteenth AF was activated in Tunis, under Gen. James "Jimmy" Doolittle's command. The Fifteenth took up the strategic bombardment role in the Mediterranean, launching B-24s and B-17s the next day to Wiener-Neustadt.

Armistice Day, November 11—a day commemorating the end of World War I, and symbolizing world peace—was greeted in 1943 by a busy slate of B-24 operations around the world. Six Fourteenth AF B-24s bombed the Burma Road, causing a punishing landslide. Twenty-eight B-24s from Fifteenth AF units attacked the Annecy ball bearing plant and a viaduct at Antheor, both in southern France. Meanwhile, Fifth AF B-24s bombed Lakunai airfield, and the Thirteenth joined planes from the Fifth AF, US Navy aircraft carriers, and the Royal Australian Air Force (RAAF) in an attack on Rabaul Harbor—the first Rabaul strike for elements of the Thirteenth. In the central Pacific, the Seventh AF was on the receiving end of an attack as Japanese bombers hit the Nanumea airfield, damaging or destroying several planes including one B-24.

On November 15 and 16, the Fourteenth AF persisted in strikes on the Hong Kong-Kowloon areas. When bad weather on November 15 kept 15 Liberators from bombing, five more hit docks at Kowloon. The next day, 11 B-24s, with a pair of B-25s and four P-40s, returned to the Kowloon docks, keeping up the pressure because shipping was the key to Japanese survival.

A telling entry in the AAF chronology for the last day of November 1943 chronicled a force of 200 Eighth AF heavy bombers that aborted their mission because of cloud formations which made it difficult for the bombers to form up over England, and which, according to the Air Force chronology, required "flying at altitudes not feasible for the B-24s included in the mission." (As detailed in another chapter of this

book, the increasing weight of B-24s equipped for combat in the European environment levied a penalty in altitude performance.)

On the third of December, Fifteenth AF B-24s bombed Rome.

After the withdrawal of Japanese forces from the Aleutians, Liberator activity in Alaska diminished. But on December 8, three Eleventh AF B-24s flew an armed recon mission, while that night, another B-24 sent on a photo mission over Kasatochi Island turned back with mechanical problems.

December 13, 1943, was the first time the Eighth AF put up more than 600 heavy bombers on a single mission, when a total of 649 B-17s and B-24s, out of 710 originally dispatched, dropped bombs on German port areas at Hamburg and Bremen, and subma-

*Fifth BG B-24s depart smoking refineries at Balikpapan.* Jack Hayes Collection

rine yards at Kiel. Also for the first time, P-51 Mustang fighters escorting the bombers reached the limit of their escort range.

The night of December 19 reverberated with the engines of 20 B-24s sent by Tenth AF units to bomb newly expanded docks in Bangkok. Substantial damage was claimed.

On December 21, eight Seventh AF B-24s from Nanumea conspired with four Navy PB4Y-1s on a photo mission over Kwajalein Atoll in the Marshall Islands. (Sometimes, the battle order called for the AAF B-24s to bomb the target, keeping enemy defenses occu-

B-24s of the 5th and 307th BGs attack a Japanese surface fleet in Brunei Bay in northern Borneo on November 16, 1944. Intense, long-range flak downed several Liberators; warship near bottom center of photo is illuminated by its own muzzle blasts reflecting off the water. Jack Hayes Collection

pied, while the Navy patrol bombers photographed enemy installations from slightly farther away, relatively unhindered.)

The official history highlighted a Fifth AF mission by B-24s the night of December 23–24, in which the Liberator crews harassed Japanese forces at Cape Gloucester by dropping small bombs, hand grenades, and beer bottles. (The use of empty beer bottles was not limited to this one particular B-24 mission. Some crews found they could drop empty beer bottles that would whistle as they fell, creating the illusion of a bomb in flight. When no explosion resulted, the crews reasoned, the enemy would be wary of delayed-action bombs; a cheap way of stretching limited resources.)

Christmas Day 1943 saw the Fifth AF mount a mission of about 180 B-26s, B-25s, A-20s, and B-24s against Cape Gloucester, continuing bombing pressure on that target as an ongoing pre-invasion softening, under way for days. The day after Christmas, the US 1st Marine Division landed at the cape.

Over Italy on December 28, 17 unescorted B-24s from Fifteenth AF units were jumped by about 50 fighters before reaching their target: the marshaling yards at Vicenza. Ten B-24s were shot down. Several B-24s salvoed their bombs over the target area. The Liberators claimed 18 fighters shot down. That same day, in the central Pacific, the Seventh AF exemplified island-hopping by staging B-24s out of Tarawa to hit Maloelap. Not too much

earlier in the year, Tarawa itself was the target of the Seventh Liberators.

On the last day of 1943, a year that saw B-24 strength swell in all theaters where they were used, the Fourteenth AF launched 25 Liberators against the Lampang railroad yards. Large fires and many secondary explosions were noted.

Activation of the 868th BS, working directly under XIII Bomber Command, took nocturnal, radar-equipped Snooper SB-24s out of the domain of the 5th BG effective January 1, 1944. Snoopers flew night interdiction missions against targets including Japanese shipping.

The Eighth AF sent more than 570 B-17s and B-24s over Germany on January 11. Electronics-equipped Pathfinder aircraft in the formation included, for the first time, B-24s. This textbook European strategic bombing mission was contested by 500 German fighters; 60 heavy bombers went down.

Single B-24 armed recon sorties bombed Maliai, Vunakanau, and Lakunai on January 18, 1944. The growing strength of the Fifth AF B-24 bomb groups manifested itself January 19 when 57 Liberators bombed Boram, while 17 more hit Amboina and Halong, and two more claimed hits on a freighter near Aitape. Sixteen Tenth AF B-24s bombed an encampment at Prome, Burma, on January 22. The Seventh AF kept up a program of bombing Kwajalein after staging through Tarawa during this period in the war. Fifteenth AF B-24s took the war to enemy marshaling yards and other transportation targets in Italy during this time.

Bombing by the light of flares dropped by other B-24s, 19 Liberators of Thirteenth AF units attacked the Japanese-held airstrip at Lakunai late in the evening of January 25. Forty-three Eighth AF B-24s, using Gee-H blind-bombing equipment for the first time, bombed a V-weapon site at Bonnieres on January 28. Gee-H was more accurate than the older H2X system, but was tethered to a 200mi range for its homing beacon.

On January 29, with American invasion troops heading toward the Marshall Islands, Seventh AF B-24s kept up day and night attacks on Maloelap, Jaluit, Aur Atoll, Wotje, and Mille. The next night, they kept up all-night air strikes against Kwajalein, readying for the invasion of that atoll on the last day of January by US Army and Marine troops. On the first of February, the Seventh AF deployed B-24s to hit beach defenses on Kwajalein to aid the American troops fighting there. On February 2, 1944, Fifteenth AF B-24s bombed a radar station at Durazzo in northern Albania. Spitfires escorted the Liberators over Italy.

Eleventh AF B-24s joined P-38s and Navy aircraft to fly cover missions for Navy destroyers and light cruisers retiring after bombarding the Kurabu Cape-Musashi Bay areas. The planes then photographed and attacked Paramushiru and Shimushu in the Kuril Islands.

The 454th BG's B-24s became operational with the Fifteenth AF on February 8, 1944, bringing the total of heavy bomb groups in the Fifteenth to 10. The 455th and 456th B-24 groups added their strength to the Fifteenth when they went operational on February 18. Two days later, Fifteenth AF B-24s bombed enemy troop concentrations at the Anzio beachhead.

On February 14, 1944, the Seventh AF put up more than 40 B-24s of the 11th and 30th BGs, launching from Makin and Tarawa, and striking Ponape Island during the first Seventh AF raid in the Caroline Islands. Two of the B-24s bombed the alternate target at Emidj Island.

During February, the Eighth AF B-24s repeatedly bombed German V-weapon sites. Additionally, Eighth B-24s struck other targets. On February 24, 238 Liberators bombed an airfield and factory at Gotha, suffering a loss of 33 B-24s. A combined force of 680 B-17s and B-24s from the Eighth bombed aircraft factories at Regensburg, Augsburg, and Furth, as well as a ball bearing producer at Stuttgart on February 25. The attacks were launched in concert with a Fifteenth AF raid on Regensburg, and significant attacks by the RAF on Schweinfurt and Augsburg the nights of February 24–25 and February 25–26, respectively. The two European strategic bombardment forces—the Eighth and Fifteenth AFs—continued to set the pace for massive deployments of B-24s against strategic daylight targets.

On February 26, XI Bomber Command (Air Striking Group TG 90.1) was directed to perform armed photo recon missions in the Kurils by day or by night, as weather permitted in the harsh northern regions.

In the Pacific, the presence of substantial numbers of B-24s was sometimes a wearying signal to the Japanese that another Allied invasion was at hand. On February 28, 1944, 23 Fifth AF B-24s and 39 A-20s bombed Hansa Bay, New Guinea. About 20 other Liberators bombed the nearby Awar and Nubia airfields. A mixed group of B-25s and B-24s hit Momote, Lorengau, and other targets in the Admiralty Islands in preparation for the Allied landing.

Entries for early March 1944 continued the almost daily use of Liberators on varied fronts. The harsh Alaskan environment forced nine Eleventh AF B-24s to turn back to Shemya, in the Aleutians, from a search for enemy shipping on March 3, as heavy icing and squalls thwarted the Liberators. Two days later, obstructive cloud conditions caused many aborts in a 219-plane Eighth AF B-24 mission to bomb airfields in France. Alternate targets were bombed by the remaining B-24s. On March 11, 34 Eighth B-24s bombed the V-weapon site at Wizernes, using blind-bombing techniques be-

*A 5th BG B-24 conformed to the drainage ditch beside the runway in this mishap. Sharp pieces of runway coral could puncture tires, leading to results similar to this. Harvey Davison Collection*

cause of a thick overcast. The next day, 52 Eighth AF Liberators again used blind-bombing techniques to bomb the V-weapon site at Saint-Pol/Siracourt. On March 9, while approximately 300 B-17s bombed Berlin, Eighth AF B-24s numbering 158 laid bombs on other targets, including Hannover, Brunswick, and Nienberg.

Seventh AF B-24s operated out of Kwajalein for the first time on March 11, 1944, on the first raid from the Marshall Islands against Wake. Four days later, the Seventh again capitalized on its positioning at Kwajalein to send B-24s on its first mission against Truk Atoll, striking Dublon and Eten Islands in a predawn raid that also saw alternate targets at Oroluk Anchorage and Ponape Town hit.

As March 1944 wore on, Thirteenth AF B-24s added their weight to repeated strikes on Rabaul.

March 15 saw the contested area around Monte Cassino, in central Italy, bombed by a mixture of more than 300

The Goon *immortalized a nemesis of Popeye, and flew combat over China. The plane is B-24D number 41-24183.* US Air Force via Jeff Ethell Collection

Fifteenth AF B-24s and B-17s, supporting the US Fifth Army. On March 17, bombs from more than 200 Fifteenth AF B-24s whistled down on Vienna and targets of opportunity, as P-47s and P-38s provided escort cover. That same day, Fifth AF Liberators continued their campaign against Wewak, New Guinea. Two days later, the Fifth launched 130 aircraft, including B-24s, B-25s, A-20s, and P-38s, to attack and nearly annihilate a Japanese supply convoy trying to make it from Wewak to Hollandia; at least five ships were sunk.

About 650 Eighth AF B-24s and B-17s attacked the Berlin vicinity on March 21, while 56 Eighth B-24s went after the V-weapon launch facility at Watten. That same day, the Thirteenth AF put up 22 B-24s to bomb Vunakanau airfield. The pattern for B-24 attacks in the Pacific in this era showed a willingness to deploy large formations when called for, or to use small groups or single Liberators on less dense targets, sometimes at night, contrary to doctrine in place over Europe.

On March 25, six Fourteenth AF B-24s dropped bombs on a motor pool and fuel dump at Mangshih in western China, taking out a large portion of the target area.

In the spring of 1944, Allied troops were pressed in by Japanese forces in the Imphal Valley in India. The situation called for drastic measure, including rushing C-47 units from Italy to India to help airlift supplies to the surrounded garrison. On March 26, 1944, three Tenth AF Liberators and an equal number of B-25s bombed Japanese troops along the Imphal-Tiddim Road.

An increasing number of Fifteenth AF heavy bomb groups led to the largest attack by that Air Force to date, on March 28, when almost 400 B-24s and B-17s bombed marshaling yards at Verona and Mestre, and railroad and highway bridges at Cesano and Fano. None of the heavy bombers were lost, while their gunners, and excellent fighter escorts, claimed 12 enemy fighters downed for the loss of five American fighters. The following day,

an even larger Fifteenth AF total, still hovering around 400 B-24s and B-17s, bombed marshaling yards at Turin, Bolzano, and Milan.

While the Fifteenth AF set and broke records in Italy, the Tenth AF continued to slug away at Japanese-held targets, putting up a dozen Liberators to bomb the Victoria Lake area near Rangoon on March 29. That same day, B-24s of the Thirteenth AF's 307th BG made the first daylight raid on Truk Atoll, when they hit the airfield on Eten Island. The complex mission staged from Munda through Torokina for arming and Nissan for refueling. Unescorted, the B-24s made claims for 31 Japanese interceptors destroyed, as well as about 50 aircraft on the ground. Two of the Long Rangers' Liberators were casualties on the mission.

March 30 saw the Fifth AF flex its increasing muscles with a show of more than 60 B-24s, backed up by about 90 P-47s and P-38s, conducting the first large-scale daylight raid on Hollandia. Airfields and fuel dumps were targeted. The fighter screen protecting the B-24s claimed 10 kills that day. The Fifth sent more than 60 Liberators back to Hollandia the next day, continuing a familiar pattern of pressure on Japanese strongholds.

On the first of April 1944, heavy clouds covered the path of 438 B-24s and B-17s sent by the Eighth AF to bomb Europe's largest chemical complex at Ludwigshafen in southern Germany. The 192 B-17s in the lead force abandoned the mission over the French coast in the face of the clouds. The second force's 246 B-24s became dispersed as they pressed the attack. Liberators numbering 162 bombed targets of opportunity at Pforzheim and Grafenhausen; another 26 B-24s inadvertently bombed Schaffhausen, in neutral Switzerland, and Strasbourg, France, mistaking them for German towns.

On April 3, a trio of Fourteenth AF B-24s sowed mines in Haiphong Harbor.

The Fifteenth AF sent 334 B-24s and B-17s to bomb Ploesti and other targets on April 5, 1944. Enemy fighters and antiaircraft shot down a total of 13 of the mixed heavy bombers. That same day, the Tenth AF sent 13 B-24s to bomb the railroad in Burma from

Moulmein to Kanchanaburi, destroying three bridges and damaging several more. Tracks and railroad cars also suffered under the B-24 attack.

On April 10, the Fifth AF put about 60 B-24s into the air to team with American destroyers, bombing Hansa Bay, and concentrating on antiaircraft positions and airfields, setting the stage for subsequent raids by a variety of Fifth AF warplanes on days to follow.

The Eleventh AF sent three Liberators to photograph and bomb Matsuwa Island on April 11; two of the B-24s turned back while the third bombed Matsuwa's runway area. Two days later, three Eleventh Liberators again visited Matsuwa and Onekotan Islands. The next day, three B-24s added Paramushiru Island to the list while again flying armed recon over Matsuwa and Onekotan.

April 15 saw yet another Fifteenth AF attack on Ploesti, Bucharest, and Nish, with a large mixed group totaling 448 B-24s and B-17s. The inaugural Seventh AF raid on the Mariana Islands was an April 18, 1944, B-24 mission in which B-24s escorted US Navy photo recon aircraft investigating Saipan.

Inclement weather forced the recall of Fifteenth AF bombers on April 21; of 17 bomb groups originally dispatched, seven groups did not receive the recall signal. More than 100 B-24s ended up over Bucharest and Turnu-Severin. Of 150 friendly fighters sent out as escorts, more than 40 rendezvoused with the unrecalled B-24s, and engaged about 30 enemy fighters. The other fighters, not meeting up with bombers to escort, attacked about 40 enemy fighters. When the day was over, the fighters and B-24s claimed 35 aerial victories for the loss of 10 American warplanes.

The Fifteenth and Eighth AFs interacted on April 24, when more than 520 Fifteenth AF B-24s and B-17s, escorted by more than 250 fighters, attacked Bucharest and Ploesti, occupying many enemy fighters. At the same time, the Eighth sent 716 B-24s and B-17s over a variety of German targets. Even with Fifteenth AF pressure, the Luftwaffe concentrated 250 fighters on the Eighth AF fleet. The Eighth lost a

staggering total of 39 B-24s and B-17s on this day.

The Seventh AF launched its first mission against Guam on the night of April 24–25 when Kwajalein-based B-24s, staging through Eniwetok Atoll, struck Truk and Guam. On the last day in April, the Seventh mustered 41 Kwajalein-based Liberators to bomb a variety of targets at Wake Island.

The Tenth AF put more than 30 B-24s over Mandalay, Maymyo, and Yenangyaung's oil facility on May Day 1944, as the Thirteenth sent out 24 B-24s over coastal guns at Borpop; the Thirteenth Air Task Force sent some Liberators to bomb Woleai and Eauriprik Islands; and the Eighth AF launched a mixed fleet of 328 B-17s and B-24s to hit various marshaling yards in Western Europe. The Eighth continued its pressure on V-weapon sites during this part of 1944, often employing B-24s for the task.

The cost of running a strategic bombing campaign included the expense of launching 851 Eighth AF B-24s and B-17s on May 4, 1944, bound for Berlin and Brunswick, only to have all but 48 bombers—B-17s—recalled due to heavy cloud conditions. The toll in gasoline, maintenance, and wear-and-tear was phenomenal in an air war that often used vast quantities of resources in the effort to destroy other vast quantities of resources.

The Fifteenth AF continued to break its record for the number of heavy bombers launched when, on May 5, more than 640 B-24s and B-17s attacked marshaling yards at Ploesti and troop concentrations and the town of Podgorica in southwestern Yugoslavia. More than 240 fighter sorties supported the heavies. That same day, the Fourteenth AF dispatched 11 Liberators to bomb the docks and shipping at Haiphong, Indochina.

B-24s of the Seventh AF escorted Navy photo recon aircraft on a raid over Guam on May 6. The B-24s bombed Guam from 20,000ft, hitting two Japanese airfields and a town area before proceeding to Los Negros to prepare for their return to home base. Four Japanese interceptors were claimed by the B-24s' gunners.

On May 9, 1944, the Eighth AF began a deliberate offensive against Luftwaffe airfields at Saint-Dizier, Robin-

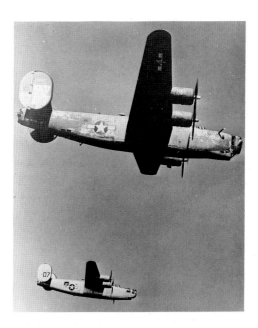

*Arctic Eleventh AF B-24s from Shemya, in the Aleutians, attacked Japanese targets. Plane nearest camera has Oklahoma City Air Depot-style nose-turret modification.* Steve Mills Collection

son, Thionville, Juvincourt-et-Damary, Laon/Athies Laon/Couvron, Lille, Nivelles, Saint-Trond, and Florennes, as well as some marshaling yard targets, to keep the Luftwaffe reeling in the face of the impending Normandy invasion. A mixed fleet totaling 797 B-24s and B-17s carried out these opening strikes.

The 485th BG of the Fifteenth AF was declared operational on May 10, using its Liberators to realize the Fifteenth's planned operational strength of twenty-one heavy bombardment groups, some of which flew B-17s. That same day, the Eleventh AF in Alaska directed its component units to focus on bombing and photographing specific targets instead of running general recon sorties in the cold Aleutians.

The Eighth AF went after German transportation with a series of marshaling yard strikes carried out by B-24s on May 11, 1944. Of the Liberators launched, 164 hit targets at Mulhouse, Epinal, and Belfort, while 24 went after secondary marshaling yard targets at Chaumont, and 66 Liberators bombed Orleans/Bricy and other targets of last resort. Five B-24s went down in the early afternoon missions.

*This 493rd BG B-24 appears to have the s/n on its tail abbreviated to the last five numerals (52496). The plane probably is a B-24H, which would have the prefix 42- to the s/n, with the 2 appearing on the tail with the last five digits.* Jeff Ethell Collection

On May 12, about 730 B-24s and B-17s—the largest Fifteenth AF heavy bomber force used in one day—ranged over a variety of targets including German headquarters at Massa d'Albe and Monte Soratte. More than 250 fighter sorties supported the heavies. The next day, the Fifteenth continued interdiction support for ground forces with a mixed fleet of about 670 B-24s and B-17s. Such raids showed a flexibility in utility of heavy bombers, and blurred the classic distinctions between strategic and tactical bombardment.

The fist of power in the Pacific saw a large force of 53 Seventh AF B-24s from Kwajalein join B-25s and Navy planes in attacking Jaluit on May 14. On May 17, more than 100 Liberators controlled by the Fifth rumbled over antiaircraft positions on Bosnik, Sorido, and Mokmer, along with supply areas and airfields on Noemfoor. Still other Fifth B-24s bombed other targets that day as the available force of Liberators grew in the Pacific.

The pressure on Ploesti's oil refineries continued on May 18, 1944, when the Fifteenth sent nearly 450 B-24s and B-17s, the majority under fighter escort, to hit those oil refineries, as well as marshaling yards at Nish and Belgrade. That same day, over the cold Kurils, an Eleventh AF B-24 on weather reconnaissance hit a Japanese plane.

The Fourteenth AF sent two B-24s on a May 19 sweep of the ocean south of Hong Kong, where they seriously damaged two freighters. The next day, 13 Liberators of the Fourteenth AF went back to attack shipping south of Hong Kong, claiming two motor launches destroyed and several larger vessels damaged. Three bombers were lost at sea that day.

In the spirit of interservice cooperation, which sometimes led to Pacific AAF B-24s flying diversionary bomb strikes to aid Navy recon aircraft, Navy fighters escorted a pair of Thirteenth Liberators as they attacked a launch and barges northwest of Rabaul on May 20, 1944. In the Tenth AF, on May 21, a solo B-24 bombed the northwestern part of Mandalay.

Clearing weather favored the launching of about 550 Fifteenth AF B-17s and B-24s on May 22 to strike communications and transportation targets and military sites in central and northeastern Italy.

Combined totals for Eighth AF heavy bombers lost in raids on May 24 was 33. During these missions, more than 400 Liberators attacked French airfields at Orly, Creil, Melun, and Poix. Pre-invasion targeting by the Eighth continued to punish the Luftwaffe on the ground. The next day, the Eighth put up a mixed grouping of 859 B-24s and B-17s, in four distinct forces, to bomb marshaling yards, airfields, and coastal batteries in France and Belgium, for the loss of only four bombers—two to flak and two to unknown causes.

May 26 saw nearly 700 Fifteenth AF B-24s and B-17s bomb French marshaling yards at Lyon, Saint-Etienne, Nice, Chambery, and Grenoble.

The remoteness and harsh weather endured by the Eleventh AF revealed itself repeatedly in mission summaries. On May 25, only one of two B-24s launched to reconnoiter and bomb in the central Kurils made it; the second aborted due to equipment failure. The next day, both Eleventh B-24s sent out on an armed photo mission over Shimushu turned back with mechanical problems.

The Fourteenth AF dispatched several B-24s on May 29, with two claiming a 250ft freighter sunk off Hainan, while three Liberators bombed the town of Wanling, and seven B-24s struck areas along the vital Burma Road. Also on May 29, the Fifth AF sent Liberators against Japanese troops and defense areas during the first tank battle of the Southwest Pacific, fought on Biak Island, west of Parai. Other B-24s bombed airfields nearby at Babo and Timoeka. B-24s of the 13th Air Task Force, under Fifth AF control, attacked Woleai and other nearby islands in the Carolines.

Seventh AF B-24s, returning from Los Negros after an earlier shuttle bombing mission, hit Ponape on May 30, as two other forces of Seventh AF Liberators rose from Kwajalein to bomb Wake and Truk.

On the last day of May 1944, the Fourteenth AF logged 27 Liberator sorties when thirteen B-24s set fires in the town of Lungling in western China, and fourteen Liberators bombed the warehouse area at Lashio in central Burma. Meanwhile, Fifth AF B-24s and other aircraft continued their relentless pressure on Wewak and Hansa Bay.

Between June 2 and 5, 1944, the Eighth AF used heavy bombers to neutralize transportation and airfields in northern France. Additionally, it implemented a feint known as Operation Cover, consisting of a series of attacks on coastal defenses, especially in the Pas de Calais area, in an effort to deceive the Germans about the location of the impending Allied invasion of France, and take attention away from Normandy.

Low clouds impacted the weather that drastically curtailed Fifteenth AF operations on June 3. Nonetheless, 36 Liberators managed to bomb the waterfront area at Ormis while 38 more B-24s dropped bombs on the port and west part of Split, Yugoslavia.

The night of June 4, Japanese forces on Truk felt the blast of bombs from Seventh AF B-24s, which staged through Eniwetok to accomplish their mission.

On June 6, 1944—the day of the Normandy invasion—the Eighth AF reached its top strength when the 493rd BG's B-24s became operational, giving a total of 40 heavy bomb groups. (Later, the 493rd converted to B-17s.) On that day the fledgling 493rd lost two Liberators in a collision on their first mission, in support of the invasion. The following day, Liberators of the 34th BG, returning to their base at Mendlesham after more post-invasion strikes, were pounced on by infiltrating Me 410 fighters. Four Liberators went down in the fray.

On June 14, four Eleventh AF B-24s flew an extensive photo recon mission above the central and northern Kurils. About 20 Japanese fighters pressed an attack, with three of the fighters suffering damage. The Fourteenth AF put up 24 Liberators on June 15 to cause serious damage to a warehouse area of Canton. Meanwhile, the Far East Air Force (FEAF) was formed, with jurisdiction over the activities of both the Fifth and Thirteenth.

Poor weather impacted some Eighth heavy bomber missions in the days following the Normandy invasion. On June 17, hundreds of heavy bombers managed to bomb targets in northern France. The fleet of 273 Liberators took advantage of a favorable break in the weather to bomb several airfields and targets of opportunity. Antiaircraft fire snatched one Liberator from the sky.

By June 20, the Eighth was realigning many planes to more strategic targets in the pursuit of victory over the Germans, as 1,257 B-24s and B-17s bombed 14 strategic targets in northern Germany. Target lists included synthetic oil plants, oil refineries, a military vehicle factory, and an ordnance depot for tanks. This same morning, another force of 130 Eighth AF B-24s bombed 10 V-weapon sites in the Pas de Calais region.

Also on June 20, the Tenth AF sent five B-24s, carrying fuel, to Kamaing in northern Burma, followed by six B-24 fuel sorties two days later, and 12 B-24 gasoline missions on June 23. (The ability of the Liberator to carry useful quantities of fuel led to the creation of specialized C-109 tanker variants, used to bring gasoline to areas where it was urgently needed, both in the CBI Theater and on the European continent.)

The cauldrons of Ploesti, Giurgiu, and Nish boiled on June 23, 1944, when the Fifteenth AF sent more than 400 B-24s and B-17s, with escorting fighters, to those targets. Opposition was fierce and accurate—more than 100 American planes were shot down that day, while the heavy bombers' gunners and the escorting fighters claimed 30 enemy aircraft destroyed.

While the crew and planes of the Fifteenth were suffering staggering losses on June 23, the Fourteenth put up 20 Liberators to bomb the docks at Hankow in central China. On June 24, 334 B-24s were launched by the Eighth to a variety of targets in France, including railroad bridges and landing strips. Of 288 escorting fighters, some later peeled off to strafe ground targets, adding to the carnage.

On June 25, 1944, the Eighth AF used its heavy bomber assets flexibly, attacking targets that often were bypassed, and using the cover of darkness in an unusual switch to night bombing. In the morning, while B-17s were launched to their targets, 107 Eighth B-24s hit French airfields at Bourges and Avord. By midday, 153 B-24s were bombing 17 electrical power and transformer stations in an effort to disrupt the flow of electricity to V-weapon sites. Sixty-four B-24s, thwarted by cloud cover over their primary aiming points, bombed a variety of last-resort targets including airfields at

Nuncq and Peronne. That night, a fleet of 300 B-24s and B-17s was sent to bomb seven railway bridges and two airfields near Paris.

A V-weapon supply site at Saint-Leu-d'Esserent drew attention from 40 Eighth AF B-24s on June 27, while 51 more Liberators bombed railyards and an airfield nearby at Creil. Five of the B-24s succumbed to flak.

July 1944 began with Fourteenth AF B-24s nocturnally planting mines in the river near Canton. FEAF Liberators bombed the airfield at Namlea and hit shipping around the Amboina-Ceram-Boeroe region, while other FEAF B-24s softened up Japanese facilities on Noemfoor Island in anticipation of the Allied landings there. Still other FEAF B-24s on armed reconnaissance bombed targets on Peleliu and Yap. The Seventh AF sent B-24s staging through Eniwetok to hit Truk the night of July 1–2, and the Eleventh launched four B-24s against southern Shimushu and Kurabu Cape, where the Liberators used radar to bomb through overcast. It was a busy first of July for Liberator crews in the Pacific.

On July 5, Fifteenth AF Liberators had the opportunity to work with Eighth AF B-17s when the Fortresses flew a return leg of a shuttle mission (England–USSR–Italy–England), and attacked the railyard at Beziers in concert with the Fifteenth B-24s. Meanwhile, the Fourteenth put up 22 B-24s to bomb a supply and ammunition depot at Canton, and five B-24s to mine Shanghai Harbor.

Flight after flight of Eighth AF B-24s—231 in all—dropped bombs on the dock facilities of Kiel, Germany, the morning of July 6. In the Pacific, Seventh AF B-24s economized on shuttle missions by staging through Eniwetok to bomb Truk the night of July 5–6, and repeating that target during daylight hours on the sixth. The Seventh AF repeated this scenario of night bombing at Truk, followed by other raids the next day, during the nights of July 7–8, 9–10, 11–12, and well into July.

On July 12, the skies rumbled with the roar of more than 420 Fifteenth AF B-24s as they attacked rail targets in southeast France. (In little over a month later, the invasion of southern France would occur.)

*Airmen congregate by a 458th BG B-24. Some of the men use the handy bicycles so evident at English airfields.* Jeff Ethell Collection

During the evening of July 14, 93 Eighth AF Liberators bombed airfields at Peronne and Montdidier; about 40 more heavy bombers failed to drop their ordnance when blind-bombing equipment did not work. No bombers were lost in this effort. That same day, FEAF B-24s pressured Yap, a FEAF Liberator target of continuing interest during this period.

A massive effort of 571 Eighth AF B-24s bombed German equipment and troop concentrations, to support a British Second Army assault in the vicinity of Caen in northern France. The RAF furnished 90 Spitfires as escorts for the Liberators.

During mid-July, the Fourteenth AF repeatedly sent groups of as many as 25 Liberators to bomb the Chinese city of Changsha.

As FEAF B-24s again pounded Yap on July 21, opposing Japanese fighters dropped startling, but largely ineffective, phosphorous bombs among the Liberator formation. In the fierce air battle, the Liberators claimed seven fighters shot down.

The Fifteenth's B-24s frequently went after petroleum and synthetic oil plants during this period, as on July 23, when 42 Liberators bombed the Albanian oil refinery in Berat.

July 28 was not favorable for many Eighth AF Liberator operations. As many as 111 B-24s were sent to bomb Brussels targets, but were recalled because of 100 percent cloud cover over the targets; 180 B-24s that were sent to bomb targets in France were similarly recalled because of heavy clouds. That same day, FEAF sent four squadrons of Liberators against targets on Woleai Island, while other FEAF B-24s bombed Laha, Cape Charter, and airfields around Manokwari and Babo, among others.

The Eighth AF sent July 1944 out with a bang, launching well over 1,000 heavy bombers against an array of targets on the thirty-first of the month. Three fighter groups escorted 447 B-24s beyond the Dutch coast as the Liberators went after a chemical works at Ludwigshafen, and the southwest portion of Mannheim. Airfields at Laon/Athies and Creil were hit by 85 more B-24s. At the end of the day, the Eighth counted its heavy bomber losses at six B-24s on the Ludwigshafen mission, and 10 B-17s over Munich.

On the first of August 1944, bad weather limited the Fifteenth AF to some recon missions, while the Eighth experienced numerous aborts because of the unfavorable weather over Europe. On August 3, 23 Fourteenth AF B-24s bombed the town of Yoyang (also called Yochow), a port in central China.

The neutralization of Iwo Jima by the AAF kicked off with a Seventh AF B-24 mission—the first to be launched from Saipan in the Marianas—on August 10, 1944, even as the Seventh's other Liberators from Kwajalein hit Wotje. Taking advantage of Saipan, the Seventh AF dispatched B-24s from there on August 12 to bomb a seaplane base, an airfield, and shipping at Chichi Jima.

On August 12, the Eleventh AF put up four B-24s and two F-7A photo recon Liberator variants over Paramushiru and Shimushu. The Liberators attacked enemy shipping in Higashi Banjo Strait as well as a runway and buildings on Suribachi. Japanese fighters rose to the attack; the Liberator crews returned with claims of three kills and 13 other Japanese planes either probables or damaged.

On August 14, the Fifteenth AF sent 540 B-24s and B-17s to bomb gun emplacements in Toulon and Genoa as Operation Dragoon—the invasion of southern France—neared its D-day. The next day, the Fifteenth launched its first mass night heavy bomber raid, sending 252 B-24s and B-17s in a predawn takeoff, to pound the beaches near Cannes and Toulon. This bombing was timed to be immediately ahead of the kick-off of Operation Dragoon.

The Seventh AF sent B-24s from Saipan to bomb Yap on August 20. This marked the beginning of a four-day Saipan-to-Yap bombing spree by Seventh Liberators.

Accurate Japanese antiaircraft fire discouraged a lone Eleventh AF B-24 from dropping bombs during a recon mission over Shasukotan, Onekotan, and Harumukotan Islands on August 25. The next day, the Eleventh sent three B-24s to Kashiwabara's staging area early in the morning, setting several fires. Seven more Eleventh AF B-24s bombed a fuel dump, docks, piers, and boats while on a mission to Kashiwabara and Otomari Cape. Again on August 27, the Eleventh went on the warpath, sending five B-24s to bomb and photograph Kashiwabara in two raids.

September 1944 opened with more than 50 Liberators sent by FEAF to bomb the airfields at Sasa, Matina, and Likanan. Other FEAF Liberators, failing to reach their original target on Mindanao, bombed Beo.

On September 2, the Tenth AF launched an even two dozen B-24s, hauling fuel to Kunming. Two days later, with heavy rain thwarting most combat operations in the Tenth AF's area of responsibility, 24 B-24s carried 32,000 gallons of fuel to Kunming. The next day, 21 Tenth Liberators again flew fuel to the city, a service they kept up daily through September 12. Then, on September 15, the Liberators flew fuel to Liuchow, when 13 B-24s formed an aerial pipeline. Liuchow continued to be the destination for several more days that month.

As land battles raged in European, the Eighth AF engaged in unorthodox missions including one on September 8 by 100 B-24s toting supplies to the battle area.

Also on September 8, the Fourteenth AF sent 18 Liberators to attack five rail bridges in Indochina, at Giap Nat, Dui Giang, Hue, Trach, Duc Tho, and Quang Tri. The bridge at Quang Tri was knocked out. Three other Fourteenth B-24s claimed a destroyer sunk south of Hong Kong that day.

The Fifteenth AF launched 45 B-24s, escorted by Mustangs, flying supplies to Lyon, France, on September 10, 1944. The next day, when poor weather inhibited many other operations, it sent 54 Liberators on another supply run to France, and again on September 12. The capacity and range of the B-24 came into play increasingly for critical transport duties during this period in the war. On September 15, while other Fifteenth AF B-24s and B-17s bombed targets including airfields and a submarine base, 53 of their aircrew flew a supply mission to southern France.

Twenty-four Fifteenth AF Liberators also began evacuating aircrew who had formerly been imprisoned in Bulgaria. The men, now free in Cairo, were flown to Bari.

September 16 saw 54 Fifteenth AF B-24s again on the supply run to southern France; the next day, bad weather thwarted all but eight of 54 B-24s tasked for a similar mission. On September 17, the Fourteenth AF put up 29 B-24s to bomb Changsha—a large number of Liberators in this theater of operations.

Nearly 250 B-24s, emblazoned with group colors of Eighth AF units, took along close to 200 escorting fighters on a sweep into the Netherlands to airdrop supplies to the First Allied Airborne Army on September 18, 1944. The Germans were deadly with their flak—16 Liberators and 20 escort fighters went down as a result.

Gasoline was vital to the onrushing Allied forces in Europe. The Eighth sent 80 Liberators carrying gas to France on September 21, then more than 100 the next day, and more than 150 the next. By September 28, the number of Liberator gas sorties totaled around 200.

Whether in demand by the Allies, or the object of attack to prevent its use by the Axis, petroleum was essential to the war effort. On the last day of September 1944, FEAF-directed B-24s bombed Japanese-held oil production facilities at Balikpapan, Borneo—called the Ploesti of the Pacific. FEAF Liberators returned to Balikpapan on October 3, and again on October 10 and 14.

The Seventh AF continued paying calls on persistent targets in the central Pacific. On October 4, it sent Liberators from Saipan to attack shipping west of Iwo Jima, and to bomb airfields, buildings, a radio station, and area targets on Pagan, Marcus, and Iwo Jima. Meanwhile, other Seventh AF B-24s from the Marshalls dropped bombs on the airfield at Moen.

FEAF B-24s roared over Mindanao to bomb Zamboanga on October 7; escorting P-38s exercised by hitting seaplanes, shipping, and targets of opportunity in the area.

Also on October 10, four B-24s of the plucky Eleventh AF were forced to abort a strike aimed at Kashiwabara

*Bombs await loading and mating with fins for this 460th BG B-24 in Italy. Tailored covers protected glazed areas of the B-24 on the ground. Jeff Ethell Collection*

because of weather. Two days later, the Eleventh got three B-24s off to bomb airfield and shipping targets around Matsuwa and Onekotan. On October 12, four Eleventh AF B-24s bombed and photographed targets at Kashiwabara.

Twenty-eight B-24s were part of a force including 33 P-51s and 18 P-40s dispatched by units of the Fourteenth AF to bomb White Cloud airfield and shipping near Hong Kong on October 15; two Fourteenth B-24s also bombed Amoy that day. Strafing was executed by a lone Eleventh AF B-24, attacking a freighter off Shimushiru on October 16. The following day, the Eleventh AF put up seven B-24 sorties—a sizable number for Aleutian operations. These Liberators flew cover for a naval task force.

FEAF's main effort for October 17, 1944, was a strike by nearly 60 B-24s on barracks, shore targets, and oil installations on Ilang and northern Davao Bay in the Philippines.

A lone radar-equipped Snooper SB-24 dispatched by the Seventh AF

dropped bombs, at Iwo Jima, the night of October 20–21. On October 21, 28 Seventh AF B-24s from Saipan bombed Iwo Jima, continuing the pressure on the Japanese there. It was a busy period for Seventh Liberators—2 more B-24s bombed Yap that day, in the first American air strike launched from Guam.

Successes in the ongoing Allied prosecution of the European war diminished the need for covert supply-dropping Carpetbagger B-24s, as major portions of France were retaken from German forces. On October 22, the 492nd BG and its Carpetbagger B-24s, which had been under control of VIII Fighter Command, were reassigned to 1st Bomb Division for employment as an anomalous (for the Eighth AF) night-bombing group. A remaining Carpetbagger squadron would continue to resupply underground forces in Scandinavia, the Low Countries, and Germany, until VE-Day.

On October 28, FEAF Liberators struggled with bad weather to bomb the airfield at Puerta Princesa in the Philippines. The night of October 28–29, FEAF B-24s bombed the dock area at Wilhelmina.

Weather dismantled a major Fifteenth AF operation on October 29, when only 35 B-24s of a force of more than 825 heavy bombers, dispatched

with fighter escort, bombed marshaling yards at Munich. The other bombers aborted missions to a variety of targets. During October 30–31, three Fifteenth AF Liberators bombed Klagenfurt marshaling yards; most other Fifteenth missions were canceled by bad weather, including a force of 174 B-24s sent to bomb Yugoslavian targets, but forced to abort due to the weather.

The first day of November 1944 saw weather relax enough for about 320 Fifteenth AF B-17s and B-24s to bomb an ordnance factory, diesel works, and marshaling yards at Vienna, as well as a tank factory, marshaling yards, and targets of opportunity in southern Germany, Hungary, Yugoslavia, and Austria. On that same date, FEAF Liberators bombed Philippine airfields at Cebu City, and targets at Alicante, Negros Island, Philippines, and supply dumps at Del Monte. Del Monte had been a frantic B-17 base in the dark days of December 1941, when Japanese fortunes were on the rise; now, B-24s were carrying the war back to the Japanese occupiers of that field. Also on November 1, the Seventh AF sent eight B-24s from Guam to attack Japanese shipping northeast of Iwo Jima. Twelve more Seventh AF B-24s escorted Navy photo planes over Iwo Jima, Haha Jima, and Chichi Jima. These B-24s bombed airfields, a warehouse, and shipping, and may have created a diversion to allow the photo planes to work without being attacked.

The tempo of the European liberation accelerated, prompting an order on November 2 for the Liberator-equipped, leaflet-dropping, 406th BS to increase its size. The activities of this unorthodox squadron would continue through May 1945.

The Fifteenth AF, unwilling to be stifled by bad weather, adapted an attack method that was tried on November 3 with 46 B-24s and B-17s, flying without escort, against a Vienna ordnance depot, Moosbierbaum oil refinery, marshaling yards at Munich, an aircraft factory at Klagenfurt, the railroad near Graz, and the towns of Innsbruck and Graz. The bombers abandoned the typical European strategic formation to attack individually, relying on cloud cover for protection. In addition to those bombers carrying out this hide-and-seek raid, 30 more heavy bombers had to abort when clearing weather—usually a boon—proved to be a bane to this method of attack.

The Eleventh AF launched six B-24s to bomb an airfield, structures, and offshore shipping at Kurabu and Suribachi on November 4.

The Fifteenth launched the largest operation against a single target during World War II on November 5, 1944, when 500 B-24s and B-17s bombed the Vienna/Floridsdorf oil refinery, while 10 more heavy bombers bombed about 20 scattered targets. They were escorted by 198 P-51s and 139 P-38s. Meanwhile, the Fifteenth sent 42 more B-24s, with protective fighters, on a tactical mission to bomb troop concentrations at Mitrovica and Podgorica, Yugoslavia.

On November 5, four Eleventh AF B-24s dropped bombs on Matsuwa and Onekotan; three other Eleventh Liberators bombed Kataoka naval base, igniting fires and drawing seven Japanese fighters into battle. The B-24s claimed one enemy fighter destroyed.

Beginning November 6, and continuing through December 24, Seventh AF B-24s on Saipan logged 24 missions in which they sowed 170 mines in several anchorages used by the Japanese throughout the Bonin Islands.

It was back to traditional tactics, if not traditional strategic targets, for Fifteenth Liberators on November 8 when 34 B-24s managed to bomb troop concentrations at Mitrovica, Prijepolje, and Sjenica; 70 other Liberators had to abort when clouds obscured targets.

Iwo Jima reverberated under the concussions of bombs from 27 Saipan-based Seventh AF B-24s on November 10; a half-dozen other Seventh Liberators from Angaur Island struck at Koror the same day. The following day, freshly arrived P-38s escorted 29 Seventh AF B-24s back to Iwo Jima, to bomb airfields.

On November 15, the Fifteenth AF launched a gaggle of 80 B-24s and B-17s to make runs including single-bomber sorties on a variety of targets. Two intercepting fighters challenged four Eleventh AF B-24s November 17 over Suribachi airfield. Damaged, one of the Liberators made a forced landing on Soviet Kamchatka. On November 21, not waiting for diplomatic clearance to be granted, an Eleventh AF B-24

air-dropped provisions to the stranded crew.

On November 20, the Fifteenth sent 92 B-24s to bomb Sarajevo's railyards, as well as rail bridges at Zenica, Doboj, and Fojnica, as other Fifteenth Liberators and Fortresses bombed targets ranging from an oil refinery at Blechhammer to a variety of weather-dictated alternates in Czechoslovakia, including the town of Zlin.

On November 22, the Fourteenth AF sent 22 Liberators to bomb Hankow. That same day, FEAF B-24s hit targets including a nickel mine in the Kendari area, and small shipping in Brunei Bay. This followed a celebrated Brunei mission by Thirteenth AF B-24s on November 16, during which Japanese battleship heavy guns successfully downed three Liberators while the B-24s were still nearly 10mi distant and approaching.

The first true long-range-escort mission by the Seventh AF's new P-38 fighters came on November 22, when 22 of the twin-engine fighters escorted a like number of Seventh AF B-24s from Saipan on a mission against airfields on Moen and Param. On November 23, 81 Fifteenth AF B-24s attacked road and rail bridges near Zenica Brod and Doboj. Meanwhile, 13 of the Fifteenth AF's B-24s and B-17s dropped supplies in Yugoslavia.

The Eighth AF's 36th BS, a former Carpetbagger clandestine B-24 outfit, became an electronics countermeasures unit, and began daily operations November 25, 1944, as a screen for the regular bomber formations. In this role, the Liberators of the 36th Squadron protected the Eighth AF's primary VHF and fighter-to-bomber communications from interception by the Germans during the assembly portion of missions. An increase in flak batteries around German military and industrial areas soon forced the 36th BS to use its radar countermeasures skills and equipment to assist the regular bomber force—a welcome aid that continued through the end of the European war. (Suppression and confusion of enemy radars remains a key ingredient in modern warfare, as was deftly shown in Desert Storm.)

Mass Eighth AF heavy bomber raids on November 26 put more than 1,000 B-24s and B-17s aloft, escorted

by the strength of 15 fighter groups, as the heavies pounded several targets. Enemy fighter opposition was estimated at about 550 aircraft. Combined heavy bomber losses were more than 35—25 of them to fighters. American fighters claimed more than 100 air victories that day.

On November 27, the Seventh AF made a strong showing, launching 24 B-24s from Saipan to hit Iwo Jima. Then, 29 more B-24s, from Guam, flew another strike against Iwo Jima, and yet another 25 B-24 sorties were logged by Seventh AF crews from Angaur, bombing Del Monte airfield. The next day, the Seventh's activities included a return to Iwo Jima by 21 Saipan-based Liberators, and a nocturnal Snooper B-24 mission against Iwo on November 28–29.

The last day of November 1944 saw heavy Liberator action in parts of the Pacific as Far East Air Force sent B-24s on major strikes against Malimpoeng and Parepare, as well as Legaspi airfield, Matina airfield, and four other airfields on Halmahera in the Moluccas. Meanwhile, in Seventh AF territory, 23 B-24s from Saipan bombed an airfield on Iwo Jima; eight Guam-based Liberators escorted photo planes over the Kazan and Bonin Islands, bombing Haha Jima in the process; 37 Seventh AF B-24s from Angaur bombed Legaspi airfield (the target also hit by FEAF B-24s the same day); and during the night of November 29–30, two Seventh AF B-24s from Guam and Saipan had bombed an airfield on Iwo Jima during Snooper missions.

In December 1944, with thoughts of a white Christmas far from home, Eighth AF crews put forth continued effort to end the war. On December 2, about 275 of its heavy bombers hit German railyard targets at Bingen, Oberlahnstein, and Koblenz-Lutzel, as well as a rail line and four targets of opportunity. More than 150 heavies aborted due to heavy clouds. About 100 enemy fighters were encountered that day, and eight B-24s over Bingen succumbed to the Luftwaffe.

On December 3, five B-24s were sent by the Fourteenth AF to deliver delayed-action bombs near the Pengpu Bridge. On the same day, the Fifteenth sent a mixture of 14 B-17s and B-24s to air-drop supplies over Yugoslavia; on

*P-51s move in with silver B-24s of the 458th BG.* Jeff Ethell Collection

December 4, 14 B-24s and B-17s dropped supplies over northern Italy where partisan activity was in progress.

Pairs of FEAF B-24s sought targets of opportunity near Langoan and in northern Borneo on December 5. On December 6, the Eleventh AF sent four B-24s to bomb Suribachi airfield, recording hits on the runway and batteries. One of the B-24s received damage from Japanese antiaircraft fire. The same day, an Eleventh AF B-24 on a weather sortie force-landed in the Soviet Union.

On the third anniversary of the bombing of Pearl Harbor on December 7, two Fourteenth AF Liberator crews claimed the sinking of a cargo ship in the South China Sea. FEAF B-24s commemorated Pearl Harbor Day with bombings of Japanese installations at Malogo, Masbate, and Legaspi. Meanwhile, over Europe on December 7, the Fifteenth AF launched 31 B-24s and B-17s on predawn raids against marshal-

ing yards at Salzburg, Klagenfurt, Villach, and Lienz, as well as targets in Wolfsberg, Spittal an der Drau, Mittersill, Sankt Veit in Defereggen, and Trieste.

On December 8, 1944, B-24s and B-29s teamed up as 89 Seventh AF Liberators joined about 60 Twentieth AF B-29 Superfortresses, as well as US Navy cruisers, in a bombardment of Iwo Jima airfields, to reduce Japanese air raids launched from Iwo against American air bases in the Marianas. P-38s flew escort for the bombers. December 10 saw a Fifteenth AF congregation of more than 550 B-24s and B-17s, sent to bomb petroleum targets in Germany, recalled because of overcast weather.

On December 17, 1944—41 years since the Wright brothers' first flight—nine B-24s from the Fourteenth AF dropped bombs in the area of Camranh Bay in south Indochina; meanwhile, the Seventh AF sent 26 B-24s from Guam and 24 more from Saipan to pound Iwo Jima. The Fourteenth sent 33 B-24s to bomb barracks and administrative buildings at Hangkow on December 18. The night of December 18–19, four Seventh AF Snooper B-24

missions were launched from Guam and Saipan against stubborn Iwo Jima.

FEAF launched B-24s, B-25s, and fighter-bombers against a total of 10 airfields, mostly on Negros and other sites in the central Philippines, on December 21. The next day, FEAF B-24s as well as RAAF Liberators were on sorties against Japanese targets. On December 24, FEAF B-24s bombed historic Clark Field in the Philippines, while three Fourteenth AF Liberators claimed the sinking of a tanker in the South China Sea.

Christmas 1944 was no holiday from war as FEAF B-24s dropped bombs on airfields at Sasa, Mabalacat, Sandakan, and Jesselton, and a dozen Seventh AF B-24s rose from Saipan to continue punishing Iwo Jima. Seventh AF Liberators from Guam and Saipan continued night strikes against Iwo Jima on December 25–26. A lone Eleventh AF B-24 dropped bombs on Kataoka on December 29.

On the last day of 1944, four Fourteenth AF Liberators claimed a freighter sunk and another damaged off Hainan Island. FEAF ended the year by sending B-24s and B-25s to bomb airfields in the central Philippines, on Luzon and Mindanao. Other FEAF Liberators went after Ambesia airfield, Dili, and various targets throughout Halmahera Island. The Seventh AF's December 31 contribution included launching 19 B-24s from Guam to strike Iwo Jima airfields during the day. Ten additional Seventh heavies flew individual harassment raids stretched over a 6hr period during New Year's Eve and into the new year.

FEAF welcomed the new year with raids including a January 1, 1945, Liberator operation against Clark Field. P-38 Lightnings provided escort cover. Through January 3, 1945, bad weather kept Fifteenth AF B-24s, along with other combat aircraft, on the ground for five days, and limited activities to some P-38 recon sorties. On January 4, the bombers were out in force; next day, only one B-24 bombed the Zagreb railroad sidings as 69 others aborted because of complete cloud cover at the target.

January 5 saw three Seventh AF B-24s provide navigational escort for seven P-38s that strafed Iwo Jima.

That same day, the Seventh sent 22 B-24s to bomb Iwo Jima in morning and afternoon raids. Still other B-24s acted as airborne artillery spotters during a naval bombardment of Chichi Jima and Haha Jima. The first use in the Eleventh AF of H2X equipment for radar bombing took place January 9 when four Liberators hit Suribachi Bay airfield. On January 13, FEAF B-24s attacked Japanese troop concentrations at San Juan, Del Monte, Muzon, and San Vicente in the Philippines. (At least one unit, the 5th BG of the Thirteenth AF, employed a spotter plane—a revamped Douglas A-24 Dauntless—to assist during troop bombing missions by 5th BG B-24s in the latter period of the Pacific war.)

The Tenth AF sent a dozen B-24s on January 15 to bomb a Japanese troop concentration and supply area at Mong Ngaw. Meanwhile, FEAF B-24s continued bombing targets in the Philippines that day, while 12 Seventh AF Liberators from Saipan persisted in hitting Iwo Jima. Hong Kong shook under the bombs from 29 Fourteenth AF B-24s on January 18, 1945.

Returning from an unsuccessful recon of Kurabu airfield January 18, one of three Eleventh AF B-24s made a forced landing in the Soviet Union on the return trip. The next day, another flew a radar ferret mission over Shimushu and Onekotan. Two other Eleventh B-24s raided Onekotan and Matsuwa.

On January 18, the 15th Special Group (Provisional) was organized in the Fifteenth AF. The next day, this group received control of the 859th (B-24) and 885th (B-17) BSs, with which to air-drop supplies over France, Yugoslavia, and Italy. By March 1945, the 15th Group was redesignated the 2641st Special Group (Provisional). As such, its units were attached to the Twelfth AF for operational control, while remaining in Fifteenth AF's sphere of administrative control.

On January 22, 1945, FEAF B-24s, escorted by P-38s, dropped bombs on Heito airfield in the first major Fifth AF raid on Formosa. Other B-24s under FEAF control-bombed barracks in the Cabaruan Hills, gun emplacements by Manila Bay, and Fabrica airfield the same day. Meanwhile, the Seventh AF, in an archetypal rendition of its ongoing Iwo Jima campaign, sent 20 B-24s from Guam to hit Iwo Jima's airfields on January 22, followed by eight B-24s flying individual strikes against the airfield during the night of January 22–23.

Eleventh AF B-24s waded into contested airspace January 23, with one Liberator performing a recon sortie along the east coasts of Onekotan and Matsuwa, and four more striking Kakumabetsu cannery, and targets on Paramushiru. Eight to 10 Japanese fighters intercepted—1 B-24 was lost, and B-24 gunners claimed two victories over the fighters.

Corregidor came under repeated FEAF B-24 attacks in late January 1945.

For nine days, ending with improved weather January 31, Fifteenth Liberators and other warplanes were unable to bomb. During the nights of January 29–30 and 30–31, some Fifteenth AF B-24s were able to drop supplies in northern Italy.

The first and second days of February 1945 saw the Seventh AF contribute to the attack on Corregidor by dispatching 20 and 22 B-24s, respectively, from Angaur for that purpose.

On February 1, Fifteenth AF B-24s and B-17s numbering 300 attacked a variety of targets; a half-dozen Fourteenth AF B-24s raided shipping off the coast of Indochina, where the Liberator crew claimed one cargo vessel sunk and a patrol boat damaged. On February 2, the plague of bad weather closed down Fifteenth AF bombing operations again, although one B-24 and one B-17 managed to drop supplies in northern Italy.

Fighters escorted 25 Fifteenth AF B-24s on a supply drop mission to Yugoslavia on February 5. That same day, the heaviest attack to date on Corregidor was carried out by 60 FEAF B-24s. On February 7, six Liberators of the Eleventh AF, sent to bomb Kataoka, aborted their mission when all the B-24s accidentally dropped their bomb loads before the bomb run.

The night of February 10–11, the Fifteenth AF conducted a B-24 supply mission to Yugoslavia. On the eleventh, FEAF Liberators kept up an almost continuous attack on Corregidor throughout the day. Corregidor and Iwo Jima rated repeat attention during this period. On February 13, FEAF B-24s kept up the pressure on Corregidor, with a sizable portion of the Liberators bombing coastal gun emplacements, and scoring direct hits on several batteries.

When weather permitted, the Fifteenth continued sending fleets of B-24s and B-17s out to pound targets in Austria and elsewhere in the region. The Eighth AF, making a deliberate effort to convert some bomb groups from B-24s to B-17s, also continued pressure on the Reich as 1945 aged.

B-24s were again part of the FEAF mixture attacking Corregidor in the early daylight hours of February 16, followed later in the day by amphibious and airborne landings. Also on February 16, the Seventh AF launched 42 B-24s to hit Iwo Jima; total cloud cover over the island forced the recall of the Liberators. Again on February 18, 36 Seventh AF B-24s from Guam had to be recalled from a planned strike on Iwo Jima because of weather.

On February 19, a coordinated air campaign in the Pacific saw about 150 B-29 Superfortresses attack Japanese targets in the hopes of drawing fighters away from Iwo Jima, as US Marines launched the invasion of Iwo. Meanwhile, the Seventh AF sent 44 B-24s from Saipan to bomb Iwo. Fourteen of these Liberators dropped bombs on bivouac areas, defensive positions, and storage areas about an hour before the 4th and 5th Marine Divisions made their amphibious invasion at 9am on the island's southeast coast. The other 30 Liberators had to abort their invasion tasks because of mechanical problems, cloud cover, or reaching Iwo Jima too late to safely make a bomb run.

On February 22, FEAF sent 100 Liberators to bomb Japanese troop concentrations northwest of Fort Stotsenburg, while other B-24s bombed supply areas near Baguio, and still others hit Tarakan and Labuan airfields. Liberators would be frequently employed tactically to disrupt troops in the campaign to retake the Philippines.

On February 23, 1945, US Marines hoisted the American flag on the summit of Iwo Jima's Mount Suribachi. That night, seven B-24s from the Seventh AF assets on Guam flew Snooper raids against neighboring Chichi Jima and Haha Jima. Even with the Stars

*This 450th BG B-24 in Italy carried the yellow fuselage band typical of Liberators in the 47th Bomb Wing. F. Bamberger via Dave Menard and Jeff Ethell Collections*

and Stripes flying atop Iwo Jima's high ground, parts of the island remained in fierce Japanese possession. On February 25, nine Seventh AF Liberators from Guam bombed Japanese mortar- and rocket-launching positions, and blockhouses, on the northwest part of Iwo Jima. Nine Liberators returned to Iwo Jima February 27 to attack fortifications, artillery positions, and mortar sites on the northern part of the bitterly contested island.

During the latter part of February 1945, Fourteenth AF B-24s frequently swept over the Gulf of Tonkin, attacking freighters.

In Europe, 102 Fifteenth AF Liberators were launched against tactical targets in Yugoslavia on February 26. The B-24s and their fighter escort had to be recalled when clouds completely obscured the objectives. The month ended with a February 28 strike by Fifteenth P-38s and P-51s on an enemy airfield at Bjelovar, where the intruding American fighters destroyed a German-held B-24 and P-38, removing

them from any advantageous use by the enemy.

March 1945 roared in like a lion for the Eighth AF, dispatching one of its signature armadas of 1,153 B-24s and B-17s to bomb eight marshaling yards in southwest Germany, along with two targets of opportunity. Nine P-51 fighter groups provided close escort to the heavy bombers.

Also on March 1, the Fifteenth revisited Moosbierbaum oil refinery and other targets with more than 630 B-24s and B-17s. On March 6, the long bombing assault on Iwo Jima, followed by furious ground fighting, allowed the Seventh AF to land 28 P-51s and a dozen P-61s on the ravaged island.

Fourteenth AF Liberators, numbering 34 and supported by 21 P-51 Mustangs, attacked Shihkiachwang on March 8. That same day, Seventh AF B-24s continued a pattern of bombing Susaki airfield. On the ninth of March, the Eighth AF sent more than 1,000 B-17s and B-24s against an array of six marshaling yards, a big tank factory, and a castings plant in Germany. Five fighter groups flew close escort and three more patrolled the area. That same day, the Eleventh AF sent three B-24s on a shipping search that did not find enemy action.

On March 11, a day on which Seventh B-24s continued their repeated

bombings of Susaki airfield, P-51s used their newly won base on Iwo Jima to launch attacks of their own on Susaki. The island-hopping strategy continued to serve the AAF. (A last attack on American installations on Iwo Jima would be launched by the Japanese March 26; by 8am that day, the capture and occupation phase of the Iwo campaign was considered complete.) On March 15, FEAF B-24s supported US ground forces on Luzon with an attack on a Japanese headquarters area at Baguio; A-20s and P-38s also participated.

A navigational error produced a record mission for a pair of Eleventh AF B-24s on March 16, 1945. The Liberators, on a photo mission to Matsuwa, actually ranged 130mi south of the island—the deepest penetration of the Japanese home islands by the Eleventh to date. The two bombers turned north again, photographed Matsuwa, and bombed Shimushiru, with unrecorded results.

On March 17, FEAF B-24s pounded Formosan airfields in quantity, while other FEAF Liberators bombed the beaches at Panay before Allied landings there on the following day. FEAF Liberators also bombed Japanese troops on Mindanao.

March 21 saw 90 Eighth AF B-24s form up to bomb Mulheim an der Ruhr airfield, under the watchful eye of friendly fighters. The Eighth sent 235 B-24s to drop supplies to Allied forces in the assault area east of the Rhine River at midday on March 24. The Liberator proved effective in this airlift operation, using its great range, armament, and capacious bomb bays to accomplish tasks contemporary airlift planes could not match. (Some air-drop modified European B-24s had sirens installed to warn friendly personnel of an impending release of supplies overhead, veterans recalled.)

On March 28, Fourteenth AF B-24s bombed Haiphong and Hanoi docks and Bakli Bay barracks; meanwhile, Seventh AF B-24s paid a visit over the Japanese stronghold at Truk.

While a half-dozen Eleventh AF B-24s bombed Kataoka naval base on March 29, a solo Eleventh AF Liberator flew a sophisticated radar ferret mission along the Paramushiru coast.

As March 1945 drew to a close, the month's war diaries showed AAF Liberators around the world were employed against the Axis in a variety of roles. The Fifteenth AF sent Liberators to bomb marshaling yards and oil facilities, while other Fifteenth B-24s dropped supplies to partisans. The Eighth also used Liberators against transportation targets, and as air-drop planes to support far-reaching ground forces. Pacific B-24s continued the formula of putting recurring pressure on Japanese airfields and strongholds, while FEAF B-24s went tactical in a series of missions that either directly bombed Japanese troops in the Philippines, or attacked enemy supplies, support, and transportation links.

The continuing emphasis placed by the Fifteenth AF on strangling German transport in northern Italy resulted, on April 8, in a 500 plane B-24 and B-17 effort against bridges, viaducts, and marshaling yards feeding into Brenner Pass. A power-generating dam also was targeted for the heavies that day.

As tactical objectives demanded airpower, the vast armada of heavies permitted B-24s and B-17s to fill tactical needs, as on April 9 when 825 Fifteenth AF Liberators and Fortresses, working closely with the British Eighth Army, bombed gun positions and other forward military targets southeast of Bologna, immediately west and southwest of Lugo. That same date, over the Philippines, FEAF B-24s and fighter-bombers supported Allied ground forces on Central Cebu and Negros. The next day, April 10, 648 Fifteenth AF B-24s and B-17s again supported the British Eighth Army by bombing machine-gun nests, artillery positions, and infantry defenses along the Santerno River. This was the largest number of Fifteenth AF heavies attacking targets on a single day to date. Also on the tenth of April, FEAF Liberators again supported ground forces, in central Cebu in the Philippines.

On April 10, the Eleventh AF, in a coordinated effort with US Navy planes, sent seven B-24s carrying napalm with which they bombed Kataoka naval base. FEAF Liberators bombed the Taikoo docks in Hong Kong and storage areas in Canton on April 13, while other FEAF B-24s bombed airfields at Tainan and Okayama. Still more FEAF-controlled B-24s bombed the Davao area.

The Fifteenth AF broke its old record, and set its wartime high, on April 15, 1945, by sending 1,142 escorted B-24s and B-17s in two major efforts—830 heavy bombers supporting the US Fifth Army in the vicinity of Bologna, and 312 heavies bombing rail bridges and ammunition supplies and production. This was the largest war effort in a 24hr period by the Fifteenth in terms of the number of fighters and bombers dispatched and attacking, and in terms of bomb tonnage released.

Six Eleventh AF B-24s radar-bombed Kataoka naval base April 16, and one more Eleventh AF Liberator flew a radar ferret sortie that day.

In mid-April, the Fifteenth AF sent B-24s and B-17s several times to bomb in support of Army ground operations near Bologna; other Fifteenth B-24 operations during that month attacked bridges and transportation to block German withdrawal from northern Italy. On April 21, 18 Guam-based Seventh AF B-24s dropped their bombs on Marcus. FEAF B-24s ranged out to Saigon's naval base on April 23; other FEAF Liberators flew a shipping sweep over Makassar Strait that day.

The Eighth AF sent about 275 B-24s to bomb a transformer station near Traunstein, Germany—not normally a high-priority target because the Allies overestimated German electrical redundancy capabilities—on April 25. The Liberator force also had marshaling yard targets to attack that day.

April 26 saw 107 B-24s from the Fifteenth AF bomb a motor transport depot at Tarvisio, as well as several marshaling yards that were targets of opportunity. Other Fifteenth AF Liberators and Fortresses aborted bomb missions to northern Italy because of bad weather.

By April 27, 1945, the flow of replacement B-24s, as well as B-17s and P-51s, to Eighth AF units had ceased. A previous authorization of 68 planes per bomb group was pared back to its original level of 48 heavy bombers. Victory was imminent.

Six Eleventh AF B-24s returned to Kataoka naval base April 27, this time dropping fragmentation bombs. Another Alaskan B-24 attacked Minami Cape, and one more flew a solo radar ferret mission.

May 1, 1945, saw FEAF B-24s support Australian landings on Tarakan Island. Meanwhile, the Seventh AF sent 16 B-24s from Guam to bomb the airfield on Marcus, while 10 Liberators bombed air installations on Param. During the night, nine more Seventh B-24s flew individual Snooper strikes over airfields on Param and Moen.

By May 2, 1945, Soviet forces were in complete control of Berlin. Offensive European B-24 operations were at an end; the final Fifteenth AF bombing mission of World War II turned out to be a 27-plane B-17 effort May 1 against the Salzburg, Austria, station and marshaling yards.

On the third of May, 1945, the Indian 26th Division occupied Rangoon, signaling the end of the Tenth AF's war against the Japanese in Burma. That same day, FEAF B-24s bombed Saigon, striking at oil storage areas and a boatyard, the latter sustaining considerable damage. The next day, the FEAF Liberators returned to inflict heavy damage on Saigon oil installations.

May 5, 1945, a dozen of the Seventh AF B-24s rose from Angaur to bomb Koror; on that same date, a solo Eleventh AF B-24 flew a weather sortie over the Kurils. On May 7, 1945, the German high command unconditionally surrendered all land, sea, and air forces at Reims, France, effective May 9. On the ninth, the first bomb group of the Eighth to be redeployed after the cessation of hostilities began its departure from Old Buckenham in England to the United States. It was the B-24-equipped 453rd BG: the only bomb group departing by ship.

Because radar returns uncovered considerable Japanese shipping activity between Paramushiru and Shimushu, on May 9 a dozen Eleventh AF B-24s radar-bombed through overcast in an effort at thwarting the operation. Another B-24 flew a radar ferret mission over Paramushiru and Shimushu.

On the ninth of May, the Seventh AF sent 29 Liberators from Guam to bomb Param and Moen, in three forces, over a 6hr period.

May 10 saw the Eleventh AF and US Navy Fleet Air Wing Four conduct

*By late July 1945, veteran European Theater B-24s were undergoing overhaul at Spokane, Washington, for possible Pacific deployment.*

their heaviest and most successful joint mission to date. A dozen B-24s bombed shipping targets at Kataoka naval base, and flew photo recon over Paramushiru on the return trip. Sixteen Eleventh AF B-25 Mitchell medium bombers also hit targets that day; one B-25 and one B-24 made forced landings in the Soviet Union. On May 15, the Eleventh sent 13 B-24s to bomb the Kashiwabara-Kataoka area; the Liberators claimed one ship destroyed and another taking a direct hit. Japanese antiaircraft fire punched into two of the B-24s, one of which limped to a forced landing in the Soviet Union. Eleventh Liberators flew other strikes as May progressed.

On May 20, FEAF B-24s bombed Piso Point, and Seventh AF Liberators from Guam attacked a Japanese air operations building on Marcus. The ensuing days of May were sprinkled with Pacific B-24 missions, like a 26-ship attack on the Marcus airfield and environs by the Seventh AF B-24s on May 24; FEAF B-24s pounding railyards and rolling stock east of Saigon at

Muong Man and Phan Rang on May 27 and 28; and a large force of more than 100 FEAF Liberators attacking Kiirun and several other towns on Formosa on May 29. FEAF ended May with several days of B-24 efforts using about 100 bombers to execute.

On June 2, FEAF B-24s struck the Pontianak airfield, and Tarakan and Labuan Islands. Pontianak harbored a wooden-boat industry useful to the Japanese, and its airfield provided at least rudimentary defense, as Navy Liberator crews learned when challenged there. The third of June, a lone Fourteenth AF B-24, with two P-51s as escorts, damaged a bridge north of Shihkiachwang.

Three years after the Japanese had launched serious air attacks against American installations in the Aleutians, the Eleventh AF sent 11 B-24s to radar-bomb the Japanese at Kataoka naval base on June 4, 1945. The ongoing dependency of Pacific combatants on ships was underscored by a June 7 attack by two dozen Seventh AF B-24s on a boat repair basin on Aurapushekaru Island.

On June 9, the Eleventh AF sent six B-24s and eight B-25s to work with US Navy surface and air units attacking the Kurils. The Liberators did not score results that day, half of them jettisoning their bomb loads.

An Eleventh B-24 flew the theater's longest mission, lasting 15.5hr, and having a round-trip distance of 2,700mi, on June 19. This shipping search mission took the Liberator as far as Uruppu Island. Turning north, the B-24 dropped bombs on a small convoy 25mi southwest of Shimushu Bay, sinking one vessel, damaging another, and torching two more.

For 19 days running, from June to July 1, 1945, FEAF Liberators bombed parts of the Balikpapan oil refinery complex and especially its defenses, in the time-honored Pacific tradition of pulverizing a target with relentless bombings prior to an invasion. Australian forces made amphibious landings on Balikpapan on July 1; FEAF B-24 attacks there continued to accumulate after the landings, at least as late as July 9, the date Australian and Dutch forces completed their encirclement of Balikpapan Bay. On July 8, FEAF B-24 attacks included some RAAF Liberators bombing warehouses at Donggala.

The securing of Okinawa allowed the Seventh AF to put B-24s there; on July 9, 43 Liberators left Okinawa to bomb Omura airfield while another B-24 hit the airfield on Kikai Island. The next day, 43 Okinawa-based B-24s bombed Wan and Sateku airfields on Kikaiga Island. From July 11–14, FEAF B-24s pounded troop concentrations on Negros Island, supporting Allied troops with these tactical operations. As FEAF B-24s gained footholds closer to their targets, they stretched their war to China, as on July 18 when a gaggle of bombers and fighters paid a visit to the Shanghai area. The biggest and most successful Eleventh mission of the month came on July 20, when eight B-24s bombed hangars and revetments on Matsuwa airfield.

The Fifth AF shared in the use of Okinawa, as more than 100 of the Fifth's FEAF-controlled B-24s launched their first strike from Okinawa to hit the Chiang Wan airfield north of Shanghai on July 24.

On July 26, FEAF Snooper B-24s ranged over several targets including the docks at Pusan, Korea. On that same date, seven Eleventh AF B-24s used incendiaries in a successful raid on Kataoka naval base. As the Liberators departed their target, smoke pyres rose almost a mile in the air. Moderate enemy antiaircraft fire was inaccurate over Kataoka, to the relief of the B-24 crews.

A fleet of more than 60 Fifth and Seventh AF B-24s, under FEAF direction, bombed the marshaling yard at Kagoshima on July 27. That same day, other FEAF Liberators from the Thirteenth AF bombed an airstrip north of Pontianak. On July 28, about 70 FEAF B-24s bombed Japanese shipping at Kure, and claimed direct hits on a battleship and an aircraft carrier. Meanwhile, over Negros Island, FEAF Liberators continued to support ground forces engaging the Japanese.

July 29 saw B-24s from Okinawa, as well as other aircraft under FEAF control, hit targets in the Japanese home islands, including conventional attacks by Liberators on Nagasaki. Other FEAF Liberators bombed a pocket of Japanese resistance south of Fabrica, on Negros Island. On the last day of July and again the first day of August, FEAF B-24s returned in force to Japan, around Nagasaki. Other targets hit by these Liberators on July 31 included Sasebo naval base.

On August 6, the day the atomic bomb was dropped on Hiroshima, FEAF Liberators continued their conventional attacks on Japanese resistance pockets on Negros Island. Two days later, in a move some American planners thought was opportunistic, the Soviet Union declared war on Japan. FEAF B-24s over Honshu bombed Iwakuni airfield on August 9, the day an atomic bomb was dropped by a B-29 over Nagasaki.

Through August 13, Pacific B-24s continued bombing missions. The Eleventh AF launched its last combat mission on that date, when a half-dozen B-24s radar-bombed Kashiwabara's staging area, leaving behind towering columns of smoke. That same date, FEAF B-24s and B-25s flying out of Okinawa pounded Japanese shipping in the waters by Korea and Kyushu, as well as in the Inland Sea.

On August 21, days after the August 15 cessation of offensive action against Japan, two Eleventh AF Liberators attempted to photograph the Soviet occupation of the Kurils, but were thwarted by cloud cover. Four more of its B-24s aborted a photo mission to

Paramushiru and Shimushu because of weather; this latter mission was successfully completed on August 23. On the twenty-fourth, Eleventh AF B-24s again failed to photograph the Soviet occupation of the Kurils because of clouds.

The stage was being set for the Cold War as two Eleventh AF B-24s flew a high-altitude photo recon mission of Paramushiru and Shimushu on September 4, 1945, and encountered Soviet fighters. (Liberator historian Rhodes Arnold says Eleventh AF B-24s were confronted by Lend-Lease P-63 Kingcobras in Soviet markings on at least one occasion.) On September 6, all further Eleventh AF missions of a wartime nature were canceled.

This chronology of the Liberator's war cannot detail every mission by every B-24; nor can it relate all the courage, ingenuity, and suffering that went into these massive Liberator efforts around the world. But it does show the rise and fall of the Axis, and the continuing rise of the USAAF, pushed ahead in no small part by the successes enjoyed by Liberator crews, from late 1941 well into 1945.

*Chapter 3*

# Submarines and Repatriates

## The AAF Stalks a Submarine

A year into the war, an AAF antisubmarine B-24D under the umbrella of VIII Bomber Command left its English base at St. Eval, at 8:45am on the last day of 1942. The stout Liberator was part of the 1st Antisubmarine Squadron, in an era when the AAF claimed these long-ranging missions for its Liberators. Exactly 5hr, 1min later, as the lone Liberator droned over the waves at 1,000ft, a radar return suggested a surface ship was 8mi distant, and 30deg to the right of the Liberator's heading of 270deg. The Liberator's pilot took up the trail toward the radar echo, and when 4-1/2mi distant and 750ft above rough seas, the bomber crew saw a fully surfaced submarine. A check of coordinates put the sub at 51deg, 20min north; 20deg, 58min west.

The U-boat's decks were awash, and the B-24 crew could discern no wake behind the submarine. The Liberator attacked from the right of the sub,

and slightly to the rear, roaring in at 200mph and only 175ft overhead. Using the bombing intervalometer, the Liberator crew loosed nine British-made Torpex 250lb depth charges with 16ft between each. The charges were fuzed to detonate at a depth of 25ft—shallow enough to hurt a surfaced submarine, and deep enough to inflict damage even if the vessel began to sub-

merge. The attack was executed 3min after the initial radar contact.

The B-24 crew looked for signs of a successful drop. They estimated the first three bombs in trail exploded 50ft, 34ft, and 16ft short of the submarine's exposed conning tower. Depth charges four and five straddled the conning tower; number six overshot the conning tower by about 20ft, and the rest ex-

*Highly polished B-24J-CF of the Pima Air Museum awaited replacement Plexiglas when the photo was taken in 1990. As a British Pacific war veteran, this Liberator was configured differently than its European counterparts, which were more heavily armored.* Frederick A. Johnsen

Old Bessie, *a greenhouse B-24 of US-AAF's 18th Antisubmarine Squadron, was photographed with an aircrew at* Langley Field, Virginia, in 1943. Albert W. James Collection

*One of the Eleventh AF's LB-30s, probably AL602, came to grief on a stream bank, its Davis wing's structural integrity faring better than the crumpled fuselage.* Rick Apitz Collection

ploded in the sea beyond the embattled U-boat. The crew praised the precision of the intervalometer in stitching such a precise line of destruction; the submarine was caught in the middle of the string of depth bombs. Now the submarine began to submerge; Liberator crew could see markings on the still-exposed portion of the conning tower, but these were indecipherable in the quick pass

over the enemy vessel. Up in the nose, the B-24's navigator hosed the sub with a .50cal barrage lasting 25 rounds. This early B-24 lacked a lower ball turret, so a tunnel gunner squeezed off another 25 rounds at the German submarine.

Perched in his Consolidated tail turret, behind a flat slab of armor glass, the rear gunner said he saw a "long, dark slim object at least 15ft in length rise up with the geyser of water" as the depth charges detonated. The tail gunner cut loose with 40 rounds at the object, which he later said looked like a photo he was shown of the damaged stern of a submarine. As the Liberator turned off of its bomb run, the

left waist gunner reported an oil slick in the area of the attack. A minute and a half after the attack, the B-24 passed over the spot and dropped a marine flare marker, but it failed to ignite. For the next 8min, the Army bomber lingered over the scene of the attack, although nothing of the vessel could be seen. By then, the oil slick was about 600ft wide, and seemed to issue from a geyser-like source.

Submarine crews were known to eject oil and even debris from their submerged craft to simulate their own demise, in the hope of lulling attacking aircraft into leaving the scene. The Army B-24 crew tried a trick of their own, leaving the vicinity of the attack by flying west, into the wind for 30min, and then returning, with a tail wind, for 20min until their Liberator was supposed to be over the spot. Radar did not indicate the sub had surfaced, and the crew was unable to pick up any sign of the oil discharge on the cold sea.

An hour and a half later, another plane cruised the area, having heard the first Liberator's radio report of the attack. The second aircrew reported seeing an oil slick four miles long and a quarter mile wide. Evidently the strike camera of the first Liberator fogged over, as photography of the attack was unusable.

The intelligence report of this high-seas confrontation caught the essence of lonely sea-search missions by Liberator crews over the North Atlantic. Seas in turmoil spat foam into clammy skies as solo B-24s sought out the enemy. Vigorous low-level bombing runs, punctuated by geysers from the Liberator's gunners, could often lead only to a speculative victory as the U-boat slipped beneath the waves, taking with it the secret of its survival, or its demise. This crew had more reason to believe they succeeded than some; the magnitude of debris and oil gave credence, even though the harsh elements conspired to deprive this Liberator crew of photographic proof of victory.

## Bred for Britain, Saved for Uncle Sam

The Liberator IIs built for the British, but retained by the AAF as LB-30s for American use, outlived much newer Liberators during the course of the war. Liberator historian Allan G. Blue, writing in the Spring 1970 volume of the *American Aviation Historical Society Journal*, said 51 Liberator II/LB-30 variants were retained for American use.

According to Blue, the conversion to American use (and LB-30 nomenclature) included the installation of typical B-24 style Martin top turrets on the Liberator IIs, albeit in a unique location amidships instead of immediately behind the cockpit. His research fur-

*Sometimes, bomber pilots got a chance to buzz like their fighter-pilot compatriots. Rooftops near Carlsbad Caverns, New Mexico, reverberated from this low pass. Don Douglas Collection via Peter M. Bowers*

*Feathered outboard props suggest this was a taxiing accident, with worrisome* *consequences for the forward fuselage of this B-24 at Walla Walla Army Air* *Base in southeastern Washington state.* Evelyn Howard Collection

A Ford B-24H converted to TB-24H-25-FO standard to train B-29 Superfortress gunners with remote-sighting weapons. Two dorsal B-29 gun turrets, two ventral turrets, and tail guns with radar were serviced by nose, side, tail, and dorsal central fire control gunners' sighting stations. Don Douglas via Peter M. Bowers

ther showed 15 of the LB-30s were rushed to the Philippines and Java by the 7th BG to bolster the strength of the embattled 19th BG, with 12 of the Liberators actually reaching Java. A handful of others went to Alaska and Hawaii, a few were absorbed into cargo and transport duties, and 17 were sent to defend the Panama Canal against a possible Japanese carrier-borne attack.

The Java LB-30s suffered high attrition, according to Blue, with no fewer than seven being written off during the early months of 1942. Another succumbed to a Japanese air raid while parked at Darwin, Australia. Survivors of Java joined a late arrival, number AL573, in flying patrol missions for which their great range suited them.

Meanwhile, Alaska operations utilized LB-30s numbers AL602, AL613, and AL622 out of Kodiak. One of these,

AL613, survived the harsh Alaska combat environment and returned to Convair in 1944 for rebuilding as a transport version.

In the months before American entry into World War II, some defense planners in this country quietly voiced concern over the vulnerability of the Pacific side of the Panama Canal to attack. To avoid the specter of direct US government intervention in Latin America, Pan American Airways cooperated by seeking use of airfields in the region. Ostensibly, improvements were made to fields including Guatemala City, while a newly created Co. sought permission from Ecuador to build an airstrip on the Galapagos Islands. Ultimately, a grouping of bases in several countries in the region gave sufficient locations from which to launch Pacific search missions.

Some of the repossessed Liberator IIs were fitted with ASV radar of British design. When coupled with the Liberator's great range, radar made the LB-30s viable sea-search patrollers. The 6th BG operated the Canal Zone's LB-30s, dispatching them to various fields in the search network.

As their Latin American patrols droned on, these LB-30s did not routinely roar out and sink enemy ships. Yet they fulfilled an important obligation in the aerial defense of the interests of the United States for a two-year period until the old bombers were rotated home in 1944. Just as the Japanese were forced to allocate a greater portion of their air forces to home defense after the stunning Doolittle Tokyo raid on April 18, 1942, so was the United States obligated by sound judgment to scan the approaches to the Panama Canal. The availability of the far-ranging LB-30s with radar plugged this gap, and allowed newer, more combat-ready Liberators to enter the fray in the overseas fighting fronts.

At least six of the LB-30s returned from Panama during 1944, when American production allowed their replacement by newer B-24s. Consolidated's Nashville, Tennessee, facility served as a modification center for these early Liberators. When the aircraft emerged, they were virtually C-87 Liberator Express transports, although their early ancestry showed in the circular cowlings they retained. Convair

rebuilt another LB-30 at its main San Diego, California, plant, and the seven early Liberators flew transport runs with Consairways, a contract service operated over the Pacific by Consolidated for the Air Transport Command (ATC).

The LB-30s were first cleaned with solvent before being completely rebuilt. Paint stripper was applied to cause the camouflage coat to blister and peel from the aluminum skin of the Liberator. About 2,000ft of metal hydraulic, vacuum, and gas lines were removed and replaced with new duraluminum tubing. After the paint stripper had attacked the finish of the Liberator, an air hose was used to blow the flaky coating from the skin. Removal of the 175lb coat took an estimated 50hr. The subsequently polished aluminum skin improved performance, and was said to diminish radio static interference.

New replacement wiring was housed in conduit for greater protection. This was in deference to civil aeronautics requirements, and probably helped the postwar civilian marketability of the LB-30s. New control cables replaced the existing strands. An AAF historian documenting the project said the original control wires to the tail had been routed along the sides of the fuselage. These were redi-

*The 446th BG in England flew* Lazy Lou *until it became a battle casualty.* Jeff Ethell Collection

rected overhead, which was said to make maintenance easier, while getting the cables out of harm's way when loading cargo up against the sides of the fuselage.

Instruments and cockpit controls were inspected, and overhauled or replaced as needed. Then, before the bomber configuration was altered to transport form, the fuselage and wing were jigged and measured with a transit to see if they were still in proper factory alignment. If a hard landing or other strain had twisted or sprung the airframe, it was realigned, and all critical dimensions were measured for accuracy.

The glazed greenhouse bombardier's station was replaced with a streamlined aluminum cap that opened to access a forward cargo hold capable of carrying 1,600lb. The stubby aft end of the fuselage was faired with a streamlined cone to diminish drag, now that machine guns were no longer needed there. All crew members of the converted transports worked on the flight deck, with the navigator and radio operator located aft of the pilots. A

*Arrays of 16mm movie projectors were used with an Emerson nose turret, left; a K-7 waist-gun mount with K-13 gunsight, center; and an MPC turret, right, for gunnery training at Tonopah Army Airfield, Nevada, in 1945. The trainers, probably part of the Jam Handy system, incorporated means to score students' tracking skills against filmed fighter attacks. Harvey Herr manned the waist gun in the photo, with Ken Maisch on the microphone.* Central Nevada Historical Society, Harvey Herr Collection

bunk was added to provide relief for alternating crew members during long flights.

The salient task in converting these bombers to transports was the construction of an aluminum "canoe" with 17 bulkheads and 19 stringers, skinned in aluminum, to replace the bomb bay doors, bulkheads, and catwalk keel, which were removed from the jigged Liberators. To further beef up the integrity of the fuselage, skin sheets 0.040in thick were removed from parts of the fuselage sides and replaced with material 0.064in thick. Into these thick skins, seven windows were cut on each side of the fuselage.

Some of the fuselage bulkheads were removed and replaced with stronger structure. Stout longeron members were added to the upper and lower structure of the aft fuselage to carry loads around the large cargo door opening being installed. A compartment toilet was added in the aft fuselage.

A floor with attach points for 23 removable airline seats was installed. With the ability to carry this many passengers, the life-raft capacity was doubled from two to four. Additional life-raft compartments were built into the upper fuselage in sections about 2x4ft cut into the structure.

While the refurbishing was taking place, some structure including the outer wing panels and the stabilizer were beefed up to match the increased strength of later-model production B-24s. The bomber-style self-sealing rubber fuel cells were removed, and the wing cavity was sealed to make an integral fuel tank. Four new Pratt & Whitney engines were mated to the modified LB-30s.

Upholstery in two-tone tan and white further diminished the plane's resemblance to a bomber. Soundproofing material was attached to metal members still visible inside the fuselage, and leather seats added a sumptuous look.

When released to Consairways, these Liberator airliners still belonged to the USAAF, and retained their original British s/ns for identification. After the war, LB-30s showed up in civil service with operators including Morrison-Knudsen Construction, which flew two LB-30s in Alaska. As of this writing, one of the Morrison-Knudsen Liberators that was damaged on landing at a remote Alaska strip is a candidate for restoration.

*The first Morrison-Knudsen LB-30 at Anchorage, Alaska, in the last half of 1952.* Wayne Edsall Collection

*Chapter 4*

# Problems and Solutions

## Going to Waist

When B-24Ds roared into combat, their waist gunners braved frigid wind blasts through huge open windows with low sills. Gunners swung their weapons into position on a movable post that held a fork mounting an E-12 or similar recoil adaptor cradling the gun. This prevailed well into Liberator production, when closed waist windows, still mounting a single gun each, were introduced. The first enclosed waist windows on AAF Liberators were modifications to existing aircraft. Some of these used K-5 gun mounts with E-11 recoil adaptors. Soon, the coffee-can-shaped K-6 mount, with an E-11 recoil adaptor, became the choice for enclosed B-24 waist-gun positions on production airplanes. The ultimate late-war B-24 waist window set-up used a geared K-7 mount (similar in appearance to the K-6), connected by cables with a K-13 computing gunsight and the purpose-built E-13 recoil adaptor.

At Wright Field, in Ohio, a chart of armament and bomb installations on AAF planes as of August 1, 1945, logged armament changes as they were

*In-flight view through the open waist window of David Tallichet's restored B-24J over Utah, July 1980. Frederick A. Johnsen*

introduced on the assembly lines. These tables are helpful mileposts for Liberator waist armament, although changes made after Liberators left the factories (likely including after-the-fact conversions of some B-24s to K-7 mounts), could alter these statistics somewhat.

According to the monthly armament installation chart, San Diego-built B-24Ds up to the Dash-25 block did not come equipped with waist guns as built. After the addition of .50cal machine guns in open waist windows, the next San Diego assembly line change in waist armament came when enclosed windows housing K-6 gun mounts were introduced on B-24M-10-CO machines. This was immediately followed at San Diego by K-7 computing waist mounts in closed windows, beginning with B-24M-15-CO Liberators.

Fort Worth B-24s used open waist-gun mounts until the advent of the B-24H-20-CF introduced closed waist windows with K-6s (although some former Indian Air Force [IAF] B-24J-CFs have open waist windows).

At Ford Motor Co., the first 30 E-models did not list waist armament as factory equipment; open waist guns then prevailed until K-6 mounts in closed windows entered production at the B-24H-20-FO. Next change at Ford saw K-7 mounts introduced beginning with B-24M-10-FO bombers. The hand-

ful of B-24Ns built by Ford before production was terminated also used the computing K-7 waist-gun mount.

At Douglas Tulsa, the first eight kit-built B-24Es did not list waist armament; beginning with the B-24E-10-DT, open waist guns were carried. Beginning with Tulsa's first B-24H-20-DT, K-6 mounts in closed windows were used, until the end of the Douglas production run. North American's Dallas assembly plant started building G-models with open waist windows, and never changed through the relatively short life of the North American production run.

## Setting Sights and Changing Models

The AAF's *Monthly Chart—Armament and Bomb Installations* suggests some North American nose-turret Liberators were to have been designated B-24Hs unless their Sperry S-1 bombsights and A-5 autopilots were replaced with Norden M-9 bombsights and C-1 autopilots, at which time these aircraft were to be classified as B-24Js. Since North American production totals and block numbers do not indicate construction of H-models, this substitution of bombsights and autopilots is assumed to have taken place. Some Ford, Douglas, and Convair Fort Worth, H-models also were listed with the ability to be counted as J-models with this same bombing equipment conversion.

*This view looking forward in the waist of a 5th BG B-24 (probably a J-model) shows crowding that could occur with both gunners swinging into action simultaneously. On open-waisted B-24s, hatches swung up and latched inside the fuselage. Gun mounts in the photo used E-12 recoil adaptors. Wind deflectors located outside the fuselage ahead of each waist window could be extended into slipstream to provide a buffer for the gunner. Deflectors can be seen through the windows in the photo, extended for action.* Edward I. Harrington Collection

## Project Yehudi

Slang flourished throughout World War II. If Kilroy was the name scrawled on walls and crates worldwide to signify that he was everywhere, his opposite was Yehudi, described by a wartime research organization as "the little man who wasn't there." With a sense of humor, the Louis Comfort Tiffany Foundation's classified wartime project to make a B-24 invisible was code named Project Yehudi.

Brig. Gen. Harold M. McClelland, director of technical services for the AAF, described a problem facing sea-search patrol bombers: A B-24 might acquire a surfaced enemy submarine on radar, and home in for the kill. But even a white-bellied Liberator would be rendered as a dark silhouette against the sky, visible to the watch posted in the submarine's conning tower. This would enable the submarine to crash-dive, as sailors jammed in the bow of the boat to hasten its descent to safety. If the Liberator could be rendered invisible until it was within two miles of the submarine, General McClelland said, a depth-charge attack could be made before the enemy boat submerged.

Researchers came up with a radical proposal: "If the plane could always approach the submarine in such a manner as to present the same head-on aspect, concealment might be possible by placing lights along the leading edge of the wings and in the fuselage section. It is known from data on the visual acuity of the human eye that, at a distance of two miles, individual lights are indistinguishable as such if their spacing is less than about four feet. If, by means of suitable reflectors, the light from each lamp is confined to a narrow beam visible only from the deck of the submarine, the most economical use of power is achieved."

The AAF said a sea-search bomber could hold such a constant course with a deviation of less than 3deg. Researchers responded, "Even a bomber as large as a Liberator could be made to match ordinary sky backgrounds with a power consumption of less than 500 watts."

The Louis Comfort Tiffany Foundation of Oyster Bay, New York, was given this project as part of its camouflage field studies already under way. A hashed-together 2in board studded with flashlight bulbs was placed on a rooftop 900ft from an observation point, where the Tiffany scientists estimated it represented the wing of a bomber two miles distant. A transparent blue pigment in linseed oil was painted over the lamps to "convert the spectral energy distribution of the tungsten lamps to approximately that of daylight," according to the report. On September 26, 1942, as General McClelland watched, the plainly visible board faded from sight after the lights were switched on, and adjusted to optimum intensity. The Yehudi Principle, as Tiffany workers called the phenomenon, worked! Even when silhouetted with a white card reflecting full sunlight, the test bed could be rendered invisible.

Now the Tiffany scientists were anxious to make a full-size B-24 vanish using the Yehudi Principle. The use of an actual Liberator was not practical for this next set of tests, so two 100ft tall towers were erected on the Tiffany estate, to suspend a full-size frontal silhouette of a B-24, with its 110ft wingspan and barrel-shaped fuselage cross section. From the opposite side of Oyster Bay, a two-mile observation distance was achieved. A curious construction project ensued, and by the end of January 1943, the two steel towers stood out against the horizon. Acreage was cleared of growth to enhance the view from across the bay.

A local carpenter built a B-24 head-on silhouette in six sections which were taken to the hilltop test site and mated. A defective suspension cable soon destroyed this model, and a theatrical scene-maker performed a unique wartime contribution by constructing the replacement silhouette. The form of the B-24 could be lowered with a pair of winches to cradles on the ground.

The upper half of the steel towers was painted white to reduce contrast with the sky. When elevated to its viewing position, the B-24 effigy on the hilltop was 235ft above sea level. The first time Tiffany engineers raised the silhouette in position, volunteer airplane spotters several miles away reported an approaching four-motor bomber!

Tiffany experimentors came up with the proper arrangement for the lights, as well as the proper color tint. They counseled the AAF, "Many blue glasses and blue plastics [for tint filters] transmit freely at the long wavelength end of the spectrum. When used with incandescent lamps, this high red transmittance would make red goggles an effective counter-measure." As the thickness of the Liberator's Davis airfoil increased near the wing root, the spacing of the lights diminished to provide more coverage. Typically, 16 lamps were placed along each wing, for a total of 32, with 10 more in a grid in the nose. Engineering data suggested the amount of power required to match the brilliance of any type of sky behind the Liberator.

Several demonstrations were made, the most successful of which took place on the unusually clear afternoon of February 19, 1943. Against a blue afternoon sky, the full-size Liberator shape and its two supporting towers stood out starkly. According to a Tiffany report, "...When the lights on the silhouette were turned on, the Liberator model became invisible to the observers at the Observation Post, two miles distant. The model's wingspread of 110ft occupied more than half the space between the two steel towers, so the observers had the special advantage of knowing exactly where to look. Nevertheless they were unable to detect even the barest outline of the silhouette, although they could discern the one-inch steel cables that acted as guy-wires for the support of the towers." Oyster Bay police dispatched patrol cars to keep traffic moving near the lookout point when Yehudi tests were in progress. The Yehudi effect could be discerned from the road for a stretch of about 300ft near the overlook point.

Work began quickly on a B-24 at Wright Field that was fitted with lights to prove the mock-up's soundness. During May 1943, the ghost Liberator began flights from the airfield. As could be expected, the first missions were not effective as the technicians zeroed in on the proper light alignment. Then, on an overcast day, the Yehudi B-24 made a successful disappearance, according to the test report summary. A later test on a sunny day was less than successful, however, because the color filtration of the lamps on the Wright Field Liberator had different spectral characteristics than the filters used by Tiffany.

*The lightweight B-24 tail gun emplacement had narrower spacing between guns than on powered tail turrets. This is the mount introduced on some B-24Ls. Inside the Plexiglas enclosure, the flat window may be armor glass for gunner's protection. Harvey Herr Collection*

The test bed B-24 suffered a landing accident following the less-than-perfect sunny mission, and was sent to a repair hangar. While the bomber was

*The B-24's ball turret retracted into the fuselage, with slots for each gun. The circular gunner's sighting window was two discs of laminated safety glass with an air space between the two. This window was not armor glass. Both guns in the photo have barrels removed. The barrel and internal breech parts could be extracted to the rear of the gun, leaving the perforated cooling jacket and receiver shell in place. North American Aviation*

still grounded, the AAF and the Navy reached an agreement whereby all sea-search duties were turned over to the Navy, and Project Yehudi was canceled, but the Navy used the knowledge gained to hide an experimental Grumman TBF Avenger torpedo bomber in January 1944. The post-Yehudi summary said, "In these flights, two identical planes flying side by side approached the observers over a pre-determined course. Although the conventional TBF was spotted at 12mi, the Yehudi plane closed the range to 3,000 yards before being observed." Navy enthusiasm included an order to equip a squadron of Avengers with the Yehudi mechanism.

The inventors at Tiffany said a dark, saturated blue paint on portions of the plane exposed to enemy observers might be the best compromise color for ease of illumination. They also devised a plot showing an approach to a submarine in a crosswind. Rather than crabbing into the wind, which would defeat the head-on effectiveness of the Yehudi gear, the plan was to fly an arc, with the lights always aimed at the submarine as a result.

The use of binoculars by submariners could reduce the effectiveness of the Yehudi camouflage, but the extremely reduced field of view produced by binoculars hampered overall aircraft spotting chores by making it difficult to scan the sky effectively. The Tiffany report said, "It was stated as part of the original project assignment that the use of this camouflage measure would be fully justified if its only result was to require that enemy lookouts use binoculars continuously." And should the submarine switch on radar to locate a Yehudi-equipped Liberator, that radar signal could lead the bomber back to the sub.

## Arming the Liberator

The AAF Proving Ground Command conducted tests generating

reams of documentation on B-24 armament ideas. In the balmy climate of Florida's Eglin Field, tests ranged from proof of validity for items later seen on many production Liberators, to bizarre one-shot attempts that did not bear fruit.

On April 18, 1942—the day Jimmy Doolittle's crews bombed Tokyo in carrier-launched B-25 Mitchells—a B-24C 40-2384 touched down at Eglin Field for use in lower turret tests. Only nine C-models were built before the assembly lines settled on the D-model for mass production, and it was to be expected that the odd C-models would be used for miscellaneous purposes like testing, instead of being mixed in with an operational group of B-24Ds.

The first B-24 test flown at Eglin Field used B-24C number 84 to examine a modified Bendix lower turret using an amplidyne drive, and other changes. Bendix devised versions of a lower turret that appeared in early B-24s and B-25s in the ventral position. Both planes soon deleted the turret, due at least in part to gunner sighting difficulties. Similar Bendix lower turrets showed up again as chin installations in the XB-40 and XB-41 bomber escort versions of the B-17 and B-24; ultimately, a version of the Bendix turret found a niche as the chin armament on production B-17G Flying Fortresses.

## Flexible Nose Gun Mounts

Liberator 84 also tested flexible machine-gun mounts in the nosepiece. Ultimately, many B-24Ds entered combat with a socket in the right side of the greenhouse for a .50cal gun, and another socket in the left side of the nose installed in a new window located between the edge of the greenhouse and the existing small navigator's side window. Subvariants show up in photos of B-24Ds in service with the cheek windows, with the left side window sometimes having a horizontal metal web just above the K-4 gun socket. The Eglin testers suggested the cheek windows could quickly be converted for either .30 or .50cal guns, at the discretion of individual commanders who might want to forego the bulk of big .50cal weapons. In service, the .50's wallop was preferred, and small .30cal guns as B-24 cheek armament showed up chiefly in the Pacific to bolster the frontal firepower of Liberators already fitted with power nose turrets. A few photos of B-24Ds in stateside use reveal evidence that newer K-5 cylindrical gun mounts were put in some cheek windows, although it is not established whether this K-5 cheek variant ever saw combat in B-24s.

The AAF *Monthly Chart—Armament and Bomb Installations* indicates cheek windows as San Diego factory equipment first appeared on B-24D-25-CO Liberators, beginning with s/n 41-24220. Multiple nose guns remained standard on San Diego D-models thereafter. Consolidated's Fort Worth plant installed cheek guns from the first B-24D-1-CF assembled there, serial 42-63752. Fort Worth also rolled out externally similar E-models from Ford-supplied kits, all of which had cheek gun installations. However, the first Liberator actually assembled at Fort Worth carried a San Diego s/n and no cheek mounts, since it was made of B-24D-CO parts shipped from the home base in California. Douglas' Tulsa, Oklahoma, B-24 assembly line began its Liberator production run with B-24E-1-DT number 41-28409, part of an eight-plane production block with only one nose gun. Subsequent Douglas greenhouse E-models, beginning with B-24E-10-DT number 41-28417, carried cheek mounts.

E-models assembled by Douglas and Convair Fort Worth represented knock-down kits produced in the Ford plant, and assembled at the other factories as Liberator multi-factory production got under way. When North American began producing B-24s in Dallas, Texas, the initial product was a greenhouse-nosed B-24G-NT in a production run of 25 aircraft, starting with s/n 42-78045 and ending with 42-78069. These few greenhouse G-models had cheek gun mounts, soon replaced on the Dallas assembly line by Emerson nose-turret production Liberators, still listed as B-24Gs. (Chronologically, according to Liberator historian Allan Blue, the honor of producing the first production Liberator with a nose turret actually went to Ford, with the B-24H. The G-model was built only by North American at Dallas, and introduced the nose turret after Ford had done so.)

When Ford began assembling Liberators, the first two blocks, totaling 90

aircraft, did not carry cheek windows, but the extra cheek armament appeared beginning with the first B-24E-10-FO number 42-7066.

As can be seen from tracking cheek gun installations on greenhouse Liberators, early mass production of B-24Ds and Es is convoluted, and requires more than a cursory check of s/ns if the true origin of each airframe is to be ascertained. This is because both the Consolidated San Diego factory and the new Ford assembly line produced kits that were assembled by new factories operated by Douglas in Tulsa and Consolidated in Fort Worth, until these new Tulsa and Fort Worth lines were completely established as production facilities. Evidence suggests these knock-down kit planes carried whatever features were standard at the time, on the production lines where their components were made originally.

Testbed B-24C number 84 also received a Sperry retractable ball turret, which tested satisfactorily before going into production on late D-models. This B-24C also tested a 46in diameter experimental Emerson pressurized turret in the retractable ball turret location. In this turret, the guns were partitioned off from the gunner's capsule, enabling the gunner to fly in pressurized comfort. It was the operational ceiling of 25,000 to 27,000ft in combat B-24s and B-17s that made the pressurization feature of limited value, and the idea was not pursued, even though summaries indicate the Emerson unit performed satisfactorily.

El Toro (Bull of the Woods) *showed application of armor glass windscreen and side cockpit windows, plus bolt-on armor plate, used on many Eighth AF B-24s to protect pilots from deadly fighter attacks.* Jeff Ethell Collection

Another test examined a K-5 gun mount in the waist of a B-24C. The K-5 comprised two cylinders, one set inside the other at 90deg. One of the cylinders could pivot for elevation, the other for azimuth. The gun's cooling jacket slipped through an opening in the inner cylinder. The B-24C waist window was glazed over with Plexiglas, and the K-5 was set in a rectangular frame within the Plexiglas. The closed window greatly increased waist-gunner comfort by keeping out wind blast. The testers recommended installing K-5s as standard on all B-24s, and testing them on B-17 waists as well. K-5 gun mounts did show up on a number of B-24 and B-17 waist-gun installations on combat bombers, usually characterized by a heavy ribbing to the window area.

A different B-24C (40-2386) incorporated an early version of the GE remote sighting system under development for the pressurized B-29. The use of a B-24C in this test was simply an expedient because actual B-29s were unavailable; the sighting system was not intended for Liberator production. "Picking up the target with the periscopic sight of the lower sighting station proved very difficult, and effective tracking was impossible," wrote a reviewer of the test data. In early 1943, the GE system returned to Eglin for more tests aboard the same B-24C. Bugs remained: "The pedestal sight as installed in the B-24C would not permit smooth tracking in azimuth, elevation and range," the AAF concluded. The armament testers at Eglin requested three actual B-29 Superfortresses be sent to them for testing. One would have the GE system for centralized fire control; one would carry a Sperry system; and one would revert to locally controlled turrets. (Ultimately, the GE system prevailed in the B-29, with variations showing up in the P-61 Black Widow and A-26 Invader.)

## Opinion from England, December 1942

Christmas 1942 saw three travelers from the United States touring wartime England, gathering information based on the early combat experiences of B-17 and B-24 crew members. Their trip report, filed in January 1943, carried home observations about the suitabilities of B-24Ds then in combat with the fledgling Eighth AF. The three were Colonels L. C. Craigie, M. S. Roth and J. F. Philips of the Air Materiel Command (AMC).

The combat-tested 44th BG furnished feedback on Liberator operations in the ETO. First comment in the report was a telling one: "The most serious shortcoming of the B-24 is the lack of forward fire. The installation of two hand-held guns is decidedly inadequate. Because of the narrow fuselage it is extremely difficult for the two guns to be used at the same time. They have found that the ammunition containers supplied for these front guns were inadequate."

The 44th BG's engineering officer "expressed himself as being very well pleased with the B-24 as a plane, and the [Pratt & Whitney] 1830 as an engine—because there was very little maintenance trouble that could be attributed to the airplane or the engine."

New B-24Ds arrived at the 44th BG from the United States with insufficient numbers of walkaround oxygen bottles, the AMC interviewers learned, "The last [B-24D] they got had four bottles in it. The airplane was tagged for a crew of six, which is a crew in the de-

signed gross weight of the airplane." No matter that a B-24D actually used a crew of nine or 10; it hit its posted design gross weight, with the addition of combat equipment, when carrying only six crew members, so that is how it was configured. The Liberator would forever battle staggering increases to its actual gross weight, and ramifications were surfacing as early as December 1942.

Crews quickly learned of a deficiency in the fire interrupter mechanism of the Martin top turret, the AMC report noted: "The interrupter on the top turret does not permit the guns to fire down in the space between number two and three props [the two inboard engines]. The interrupter cam cuts straight off from the top of number two to number three, about where the prevalence of head-on attacks are. This has got to be modified to permit the guns to fire straight ahead between the props." (For the low-level Ploesti mission of August 1943, some of the B-24Ds were modified to allow the top-turret guns to fire ahead and down, to suppress flak guns at tree-top height.)

## Heads or Tails: Eglin Tests Emerson Turret

The early comments of the fact-finders in England echoed universal concerns about frontal armament on Liberators. An Eglin test proved the merit of the Emerson nose and tail turret in the D-model, which showed up in production first on the noses of B-24Hs, Gs, and many subsequent Liberators. The Emerson did not catch on as a tail turret for production Liberators.

Tests in 1943 showed two fixed forward-firing .50cal guns could be effective in suppressing ground targets such as antiaircraft guns during low-altitude attacks. The big B-24 could be maneuvered nimbly enough to bring the guns to bear. However, the B-24 could not maintain the necessary glide angle—about 20deg—to keep the .50cal slugs from skipping off water, or from failing to penetrate a submarine hull. A 37mm cannon was rejected as less satisfactory than the fixed .50s. In practice, fixed forward-firing guns had been installed already in 1942 in the HALPRO Detachment B-24Ds which flew a preliminary low-level Ploesti mission, and in the Pacific some Ma-

rine and Navy PB4Y-1 and later PB4Y-2 crews experimented with field-mounted 20mm cannons for low-level strafing. (One Privateer crew member remembered the cannons improvised onto his PB4Y-2 shattered the glass in the instrument panel gauges during a test-firing.)

The problem of inadequate forward firepower in the B-24D was well known, and members of the 90th BG pioneered efforts to mount a Consolidated tail turret in the nose of a Liberator. At the request of the Antisubmarine Command, Air Service Command, and the Seventh AF (located in the Pacific, where many B-24 nose-turret mods took place), a standard Consolidated tail turret was mounted in the nose of a B-24D. A twin-mount .50cal installation in the tail replaced the power turret on the test plane; test waist gun and ventral gun mounts were tried on this plane also. The results confirmed the desirability of a nose turret, although the Emerson or Motor Products Corp. (MPC) models were requested as superior to the Consolidated turret. The testers found the hand-held twin-mount gun installation in the tail less effective than a true tail turret because of scant protection for the gunner, smaller field of fire, and lack of good balance. They recommended its use "only on missions where the saving of weight in the tail position was absolutely necessary." (Photos show that a number of B-24Ds in Pacific combat did incorporate a hand-held open-air tail emplacement, but this was not a factory option. Later, the B-24L introduced an enclosed lightweight hand-held tail armament as an alternative to the heavy power turret.)

By 1943 the B-17 was testing a K-6 enclosed waist-gun mount, and this was recommended for the B-24 waist as well. The K-6 used the K-5's principle of two cylinders at right angles for elevation and azimuth. But the K-6 enlarged the size of the whole mount, and incorporated heavy steel coil springs on either side of the mount to balance the gun (as some K-5s had also done). The entire K-6, including the springs, was contained inside the outer cylinder, which was about the shape and size of a coffee can. This cylinder, with openings for the gun, was mounted on the waist windowsill, nested into a snug cutout in a Plexiglas window. When the cylinder rotated in azimuth, it maintained contact with the window cutout, baffling the harsh slipstream from the outside. Ultimately, K-6s began appearing on B-24 waist windows.

A test M-4 gun mount with another 37mm cannon aimed by a GE pedestal sight in the nose of a B-24D at first looked promising when runs were made against a tow target at close range and low relative speeds. When a Culver PQ-8 target drone was used to make head-on attacks on the Liberator, report reviewers said "the longer ranges and higher relative speeds completely destroyed . . . accuracy." A sophisticated computing sight, possibly with ARO (Air Range Only; a radar range-finder) was also urged for this cannon mount.

Other tests tried Briggs retraction mechanisms for the Sperry ball turret, and then a Briggs version of the turret itself. Meanwhile, other testers wanted to replace the ball turret entirely, and tried several hand-held gun mounts, which had a restricted view compared with the 360deg view from a ball turret suspended beneath the plane. (Nonetheless, some Pacific B-24s employed hand-held guns in place of the turret. At Eglin, a weight savings of 750lb was estimated for one of the test designs. Data does not show what the Pacific Liberator crews achieved in weight savings or gunnery effectiveness, but photos reveal the Pacific Liberators so modified for the 5th BG had enlarged windows cut in the lower fuselage to aid the belly gunner in scanning for targets. Similar installations appeared on some stateside training B-24s.)

Jamming and vibration problems with some Consolidated turrets in action led to a modification of the basic Consolidated tail turret by MPC. The MPC unit tested at Eglin incorporated provisions for hand-operating the guns and the turret itself in case of a loss of turret power; a revised ammunition feed system; and a hydraulic jack for azimuth drive, and gear drives instead of cables. With a few modifications, the MPC turret got a thumbs-up from the Eglin testers, and MPC variations proliferated on production Liberators, as nose and tail turrets. The MPC and Consolidated turrets can quickly be

distinguished from the Emerson nose turret by the slightly canted angle of the main window in front of the gunner on the MPC and Consolidated versions.

Emerson turrets were installed in the nose and tail of a test B-24D, which also sported a Briggs retractable ball turret, Martin top turret, and hand-held waist guns. This Liberator was tested with bomb loads up to 8,000lb, and at weights up to 65,000lb. According to an AAF historian reviewing this plane's test data, it was found to be "very stable, pleasant, and easy to fly." The Proving Ground Command went so far as to call the B-24D in this configuration the best operational heavy bomber tested up to the summer of 1943.

### Rockets Slow Bombs' Travel—at a Price

A test reported in January 1944 was the use of external and internal rails attached to modified, outward-opening rear bomb bay doors on B-24D 42-40830. The installation was designed for use with VAR (Vertical Antisubmarine Rockets), or 16 60lb Mark XX bombs. The use of bombs with rocket motors was devised so the thrust of the rocket would cancel the forward speed of a normal gravity bomb, thus imparting a true vertical drop to the bomb. This was considered desirable

*A B-17G style chin turret was tested on Lil' Texas Filley in 1944, complete with B-17 style bombardier's seat.*

for antisubmarine warfare missions. According to a test summary, "On the first mission the B-24D was loaded with 16 Mk6 inert bombs equipped with Mk2, 7V-12 motors. The first salvo of four exterior bombs blew the front bomb bay doors all but completely free of their tracks so that they had to be roped and secured from the catwalk before landing." By late 1943, the Navy had taken over antisubmarine duties, and the recommendation came from AAF channels to hand over all vertical-bombing data to the proper authority, and discontinue its testing in the AAF.

A 1943 test placed external bomb racks inboard of the engines under the wings of a B-24D. From D-7 bomb shackles, 1,600, 2,000, or 4,000lb bombs could be carried. Slinging a pair of 4,000lb bombs, the B-24D lost about 25mph to increased drag; this diminished to 20mph with the 2,000lb bombs, and about 12mph with empty racks. On a test flight to 25,000ft with an 8,000lb external bomb load, the struggling Liberator took 1hr, 22min to reach altitude, when it should have made it in 36min, 30sec without the

*The B-24J/B-17G hybrid produced an aircraft with roomy nose accommodations and intolerable performance. Peter M. Bowers and Victor D. Seely Collections*

drag of the external load. The racks were not recommended for production.

## Cold-Soaking the B-24

Extreme low temperatures were sought for two B-24Ds, a B-24E, and a B-24H sent to Ladd Field, Fairbanks Alaska Territory, during the winter of 1943–1944, to see if the Liberator was functioning satisfactorily for use at extremely low temperatures. (The use of aircraft parked at low temperatures is more complex than for aircraft departing temperate climates and entering low temperatures in flight, and then returning to temperate conditions on the ground. On the ground in cold climates, cold-soaking occurs, rendering some fluids and normally pliable materials stiff or solid.)

The Liberators in this Alaska test were operated at ground temperatures as low as minus 46deg F., and at flight temperatures as low as minus 62deg F. The testers concluded that the B-24 was not as satisfactory as was the B-17 for operation at subzero temperatures.

## XB-41 Frontal Armament Raises Dilemma

In 1943 tests of the XB-41 escort fighter version of the B-24D, the Bendix chin turret was found to be satisfactory, but not as desirable as the Emerson nose turret. Herein lay a conflict: For gunnery, the Emerson was preferred; for bombardier access and

some other flight characteristics, the Bendix chin installation would be revived in tests later on.

Eglin testers quickly discarded M-5 power twin waist-gun mounts of the XB-41 because they could not be operated in the event of a power loss, and had an inferior field of fire. With the dual waist guns discarded in favor of single mounts, and with some form of nose turret on the way for production B-24s, the escort-ship XB-41 offered only the additional two guns from a second Martin top turret, plus a much higher load of ammunition, than a standard B-24 bomber variant could offer. Because the high-ammo load could slow the XB-41 down after the bombers it was supposed to escort had dropped their bomb loads, it was deemed operationally unsuitable, especially when it couldn't contribute to the total number of bombs on target.

Test personnel at Eglin suggested using the XB-41 airframe to develop a four-gun nose turret instead. Tests showed the XB-41 was about 15mph slower than a regular B-24, and could only attain 22,000ft. An AAF test summary explained, "In level flight, the XB-41 used considerably more power to stay in formation with the B-24, resulting in excessive consumption of gasoline. In addition, the airplane was unstable and had a dangerously high center of gravity." In a comparison formation test with a B-17F bomber, the XB-41 became increasingly unstable and was very difficult to maneuver above 21,000ft. (The companion YB-40 escort variant of the B-17 made it into combat with the Eighth AF where it was also discarded for some of the same reasons, including slowness with a full ammo load.)

## Hurrah for the H-Model!

Another Eglin test showed the B-24H to equal the B-17F in speed, with the H-model Liberator superior in range and bomb load.

A report from February 1944 tested K-6 gun mounts in enclosed waist windows on two B-24Js. One installation was made at the St. Paul, Minnesota, Modification Center, and the other by Ford at Willow Run, Michigan. The St. Paul version protruded outward, and centered the mounts on the bottom of each sill. The Willow Run set-up was flush except for a small portion of the K-6 cylinder, and was staggered with the K-6 to the aft of the left window, and to the forward part of the right window, to give the gunners more clearance inside. Installations much like the Willow Run version appeared on combat B-24s. Another Eglin report suggested that crowding in the waist could be eliminated by carrying only one waist gunner, to alternate between windows. This does not seem to have found favor in combat, however. (Both the B-17 and B-24 suffered from cramped quarters for two waist gunners moving about in combat. During B-17G production, the Flying Fortress' answer to the problem was to stagger the entire window openings to give the gunners clearance. On B-24s, the windows remained directly opposite each other while only the gun mounts were staggered within the windows, as described.)

Still not content with the MPC version of the Consolidated tail turret, a further metamorphosis saw the advent of the Southern Aircraft Corp. (SAC) improvement, called the SAC-7. The SAC-7 saved weight and provided a good field of fire.

Another revival of the Bendix chin turret, this time on a B-24J, resulted in mediocre ceilings and overheating engines, so the idea was dropped. Also revisited was the carrying of external bomb loads under the wings of a B-24J, which met with results more dismal than the early external bomb load tests.

## Making the B-24J Look Like the B-17G

The dissatisfaction with cramped quarters in the noses of turret-equipped Liberators led to one of World

War II's most bizarre surgeries. The complete forward fuselage of a B-17G Flying Fortress was grafted to a B-24J. According to an AAF test summary, the massive splice job resulted in an operationally unsuitable airplane. Three test missions were flown: one at low altitude for speed calibration and general aircraft familiarization, and two with full military loads at high altitude, including 8,000 and 6,000lb of bombs. The findings: "The operational performance of this aircraft is poor in all respects." The hybrid Liberator with the Fortress nose lacked directional and longitudinal stability, especially at altitude. It had a disappointing service ceiling of only 18,000ft—murder over a defended target. A very damning aspect was the notation that this nose installation "increases the already excessive basic weight of the B-24J."

Acknowledging the basically good crew comforts of the B-17 nose, the report said, "The visibility for the bombardier and navigator is excellent," adding that working room in the nose compartment for the navigator and bombardier was adequate.

## Making the B-24 Combat-Ready Again

The combat evolution of the B-24 was a series of armament and armor additions to meet ever-increasing enemy threats. As a result, late-war Liberators (especially configured for European combat) were cumbersome and overweight compared to earlier ships.

This metamorphosis was of concern at the highest levels in the AAF. In January 1945, Lt. Gen. James H. Doolittle, Eighth AF commander, wrote Lt. Gen. Barney M. Giles, Chief of Air Staff, "It is my studied opinion that no minor modifications will make the B-24 a satisfactory airplane for this theater [the ETO]." General Doolittle started out sympathetic to the B-24 in his letter to General Giles. "The original B-24 would carry a greater bomb load [8,000lb against 6,000lb] than the B-17. It would carry this load farther and was faster. Upon being put into operations in the ETO, it was found that the armament and armor of the B-24 were inadequate and in order to operate without prohibitive losses it was necessary to make emergency modifications immediately. These modifications con-

sisted, among other things, in a formidable nose turret which together with the other additions substantially increased the weight, reduced the aerodynamic characteristics and although increasing the fire power, eventually unacceptably reduced the overall utility of the aircraft. The load carrying capacity was reduced to 5,000lb for long range high altitude operation, which is 1,000lb less than the B-17."

While hard statistics for the two heavy bomber types are elusive due to a host of variables, Doolittle's letter revealed a trend toward loading up the B-24 with armor and armament at the expense of performance.

General Doolittle described another Liberator phenomenon: The lengthening of the nose, which occurred way back with the British Liberator II, was aggravated with the installation of a nose turret that protruded above the original fuselage contours. Additionally, the extra weight and drag of the turret and other additions led to slower speeds, which forced the wing to be flown at a higher angle of attack, further raising the nose in flight. With a long nose high before the pilots, vision was less than optimum, and General Doolittle said this "has been the cause of frequent collisions."

Increased gasoline consumption and reduced speed gave the heavy Liberators a radius of action less than the B-17's, Doolittle told Giles. (In lighter configurations, Liberators in the Pacific excelled as long-range champions until the advent of the new B-29 Superfortresses.) General Doolittle's letter said the modifications to B-24s had the effect of putting the center of gravity aft, degrading longitudinal stability. "The addition of the nose turret re-

Sugar Baby, *flying with one camouflaged gray replacement bomb bay door, displayed yellow bottom edges to its bomb doors common on Eighth AF B-24s later in the war. This may have been a quick-reference marking to determine when bomb doors were open, since they conformed to fuselage sides and were less visible than hinged B-17 doors.* Jeff Ethell Collection

duced directional stability and the B-24 became harder to fly," Doolittle added. "Spinning out of the overcast is much more common than with the B-17 and it is not as steady a bombing platform."

The degraded aerodynamics and heavy weight of the B-24 reduced the Liberator's service ceiling, Doolittle wrote, "until now it is difficult to hold a good formation, with load, above 24,000 feet. The B-17 can be flown as readily under similar conditions, in formation, at 28,000 feet. That means flak losses, over the same territory, would be substantially greater in the B-24."

Bad aerodynamics and weight problems aside, Doolittle opined: "Perhaps the greatest handicap to bombing efficiency in this airplane is the space restriction for bombardier and navigator in the nose and the interference with their forward vision resulting from the present nose turret. It must be pointed out that about 75 percent of our missions failures are the result of poor navigation and that inaccurate navigation through specified corridors has substantially increased our flak losses. To find and destroy small targets from high altitude, both the navigator and bombardier must have adequate forward vision."

*The experimental Bell chin gun mount tested by the Eighth AF in 1944 used B-24H number 42-7580, and the upper portion of a B-24D style greenhouse nose. Lack of sufficient parts to quickly implement this change on a wide scale, plus anticipated introduction of the B-24N, helped retire this promising innovation.* Ivan Stepnich Collection

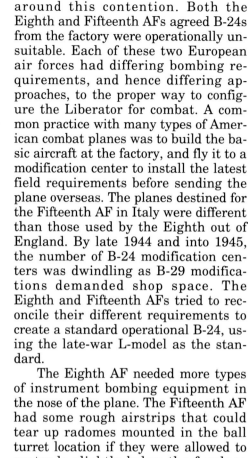

Several problems tended to revolve around this contention. Both the Eighth and Fifteenth AFs agreed B-24s from the factory were operationally unsuitable. Each of these two European air forces had differing bombing requirements, and hence differing approaches, to the proper way to configure the Liberator for combat. A common practice with many types of American combat planes was to build the basic aircraft at the factory, and fly it to a modification center to install the latest field requirements before sending the plane overseas. The planes destined for the Fifteenth AF in Italy were different than those used by the Eighth out of England. By late 1944 and into 1945, the number of B-24 modification centers was dwindling as B-29 modifications demanded shop space. The Eighth and Fifteenth AFs tried to reconcile their different requirements to create a standard operational B-24, using the late-war L-model as the standard.

The Eighth AF needed more types of instrument bombing equipment in the nose of the plane. The Fifteenth AF had some rough airstrips that could tear up radomes mounted in the ball turret location if they were allowed to protrude slightly below the fuselage contour, which the Eighth did not consider a problem. But both air forces agreed the Liberator needed to provide the bombardier and navigator more visibility up front. The outward manifestation of this was the proliferation of enlarged and bulging windows on the sides of the noses of late B-24s. (In December 1944, a navigator returning from the ETO, and a stint in the 454th BG, told an AAF Air Intelligence Contact Unit that such extra windows were vital. The alternative was grossly inefficient, and placed an additional navigator in combat peril: The 454th BG sometimes put two navigators in the nose of a Liberator, one at the navigator's table and a second in the nose turret; the second had better visibility than the table-bound navigator.)

General Doolittle argued that the requirements of the Eighth AF were more specific than those of the Fifteenth because of the greater amount of instrument bombing equipment carried in Eighth AF Liberators. He suggested it would be easier to configure

Fifteenth AF B-24s from the Eighth master copy than the other way around. In his January 1945 letter to General Giles, General Doolittle predicted: "It is believed that a study by the Fifteenth AF of the latest nose arrangement being delivered to the Eighth AF, will indicate minor changes on Block 16 [of B-24L-FO aircraft] production which will meet the requirements of both theaters and result in a single standard design pending the advent of the chin turret."

The chin turret—on production B-24s—was an experimental Eighth AF modification which General Doolittle embraced as the best way to cure the Liberator's perceived ills. The installation was not a rewarmed Bendix chin, first flown on the experimental bomber escort XB-40 (B-17 variant) and XB-41 (B-24 version). Rather, the Eighth AF modification used a Bell power boost twin .50cal unit from a Martin B-26 tail emplacement, situated below the modified greenhouse nose characteristic of B-24Ds. This chin turret, and the experimental Emerson Model 128 nose ball turret, promised to allow top contours of the Liberator's nose to return to an unbroken line, to reduce drag and enhance pilot vision. These two turrets also gave the bombardier and navigator greater working room and a better view than available in conventionally turreted Liberator noses.

The test bed converted by Eighth AF engineers in 1944 was a war-weary B-24H nicknamed *Hap Hazard*. The Emerson nose turret and the bombardier's station were removed, and the upper two-thirds of a B-24D nose grafted on, with the B-26 tail gun emplacement faired in beneath this. Ivan Stepnich, who served as a pilot and engineering officer on this project after flying combat with the 44th BG, remembered the engineers were so eager to test fly the product they neglected to clean up myriad aluminum filings in the nose compartment left over from the modification process. Since the Plexiglas fairing around the guns was normally facing aft on a B-26, it had gaps that allowed air to ram in when it faced forward on the nose of *Hap Hazard*. The result, Stepnich said, was a shower of floating aluminum bits, like chaff, in the cockpit as the wind blasted the metal flakes airborne. Cleaning the plane, and installing zippered boots over the gun slots, cured that problem.

General Doolittle said the Bell boosted chin turret was superior to the proposed production Emerson ball turret planned for the single-tail B-24N. This opinion was based on photos of the Emerson installation, which showed it to offer poorer visibility than the Bell boosted variant, while providing "no improvement in space available in the nose for personnel and for the special equipment required here for navigation and instrument bombing," according to Doolittle.

A report circulated by Headquarters, US Strategic Forces in Europe, in 1944 touted the Bell boosted gun nose, but acknowledged its introduction to existing Liberators could be hampered by a shortage of B-24D nose greenhouses to graft on to newer fuselages, some of which varied due to different manufacturers. At the time of the report, the Bell power boost units for the handheld guns were in short supply, with the Ninth AF taking priority to get grounded B-26 Marauders back in action. Gen. Henry H. "Hap" Arnold sent a message in October 1944 to Generals Carl Spaatz and Jimmy Doolittle in Europe, explaining that tests and production of the Bell modification kits would require an extra six months, by which time B-24Ns (with Emerson 128 nose turrets) were forecast to be ready, although the N-model ultimately was not ready for service by then. Arnold asked Doolittle and Spaatz, "Do you still desire kits for Chin Gun installation instead of the present nose turret in your B-24 airplanes, considering the delay involved?"

Ultimately, the B-24N was to have been the answer, but orders for 5,168 single-tail N-models were dropped after victory in Europe was achieved in 1945. When Liberator production ended on May 31 of that year, one XB-24N and seven YB-24Ns had been produced.

The Emerson 128 turret was tested in 1944 at Eglin Field in B-24G number 42-78399. It was an electric ball turret installed in the nose, replacing the standard Emerson nose turret at a weight savings of 210lb. The 128 ball used a K-11 gunsight, according to AAF reports, and provided a 120deg frontal cone of fire protection for the Liberator. The turret collected its own

spent shells and links rather than spilling them overboard as did some Liberator armaments. The retention of the shells and links was a way to protect aircraft in tight formation from suffering damage from flying debris. Especially in a tight javelin-down formation, with successive waves of bombers below and behind those preceding them, foreign-object damage from shells was a real problem.

The Emerson 128 had a unique ability to be centered and fired by the Liberator's copilot in emergency situations, according to AAF papers. Upon completion of the Eglin tests on July 19, 1944, testers in Florida said the Emerson 128 was "superior to any nose armament installation in a B-24 type airplane previously tested by this command."

In 1944, the AAF investigated ways to give the loaded B-24J a higher operational ceiling. It rejected a suggestion that the gross weight be restricted to 60,000lb, which would cut into the B-24J's fuel or bomb loads. The promise of improved performance in the XB-24N was the cause of the rejection. "It is believed that the XB-24N will show a marked increase in operational ceiling over the B-24J airplane," wrote Col. Jack Roberts in a report under the banner of Gen. Hap Arnold's office as commanding general of the AAF. Among items approved for introduction in the Liberator line was the Emerson 128 nose ball turret "in all production B-24s as soon as the turret becomes available." In practice, this effective armament was fitted to only a few test airplanes before production ceased.

*Eighth AF modifications, including add-on armor plating and bulging navigator window over the old-size window frame, kept* Dinky Duck *upgraded for combat.* Jeff Ethell Collection

Other improvement tests on B-24s were discouraged late in 1944, to give emphasis to the single-tail B-24N program. The N-model was held in high regard as the answer to many operational problems. Its engines were Pratt & Whitney R-1830-75s fitted with hooded B31 turbo-superchargers. The Dash-75 engine produced about 150hp more than previous versions of the 1830. The hood, planners hoped, would increase speed by about 6mph, and was visible beneath the engine nacelle.

The cockpit of the B-24N was redesigned with a knife-edge windscreen, which also showed up on late-production Ford-built B-24Ms. This windscreen afforded the pilot and copilot better visibility. Pilot and copilot overhead escape hatches were requested for this configuration as well.

While this redesigning was under way, the top turret in late Liberators was anchored more securely in an effort to reduce the tendency for upper turrets to rip loose and plunge forward to the flight deck in crashes.

There's a sense of disappointment that the sporty B-24N did not achieve production and never had a chance to strut its stuff—but this let-down is ameliorated by the reason the B-24N was never mass-produced: overwhelming Allied victory!

*Chapter 5*

# Warpaint

Paint and markings on Liberators and Privateers provide seemingly endless variations and mutations. Some trends emerged, and can be of use in sleuthing information from photographs. On camouflaged Liberators, deep, uniform scallops between the gray undersides and the olive uppers are hallmarks of a Ford paint job. Less-uniform scallops mark early camouflaged North American G-models. Straight, yet feathered, demarcation between gray and olive were typical of Consolidated-built Liberators.

In the decades since World War II, historians and collectors of nose art photography have endeavored to catalog the specific identities, squadrons, and serials of decorated B-24s. For a variety of reasons, errors creep into the body of information available. Sometimes, aviators with box cameras meandered off their own flightline and into a neighboring group area to take snapshots. In the years following the

*Records indicate* Virgin Abroad *was a B-24M-15-FO, number 44-50941, serving with the 529th Squadron of the 380th BG in 1945. Because airpower was massed at some locations later in the war, some confusion occasionally arises over ownership of particular aircraft photographed at specific locations.* C. M. Young Collection

end of the war, that excursion to a neighboring bomb group gets forgotten, and all the planes in the photos become melded erroneously into one unit. Efforts have been made to cross-reference most of the nose art photos in this volume. If any errors still exist, hopefully other mistakes have been rectified.

Dedicated B-24 nose-art researchers find it valuable to check multiple publications on the topic; sometimes, a distant full-plane shot in one book complements a nose art close-up in another, allowing an artist, or modeler, or restorer to render a complete version of the intended subject B-24.

## Color as Plain as Black and White

How many times have you heard someone say, "I'll believe it when I see it in black and white"?

In the case of vintage aircraft photography, "black and white" has many shades of meaning, as the accompanying photos reveal. One of the tasks of the curator, model builder, artist, aircraft restorer, and historian is to recreate the colors of the past, often with limited access to full-color photography.

The difficulty of the task can be compounded by the use of two radically different types of black-and-white films in the 1930s and 1940s. Orthochromatic film has a very low sensitivity to light in the visible red portion of the

spectrum. Thus it was ideal for box cameras where a small, circular red window on the back of the camera revealed the number of the negative being exposed. Orthochromatic film can also be processed in a darkroom with red safelights without damaging the image.

A disadvantage to orthochromatic film is its lack of natural-looking shades of gray when printed. Because red objects do not expose the film emulsion, they are rendered clear on the negative, and subsequently show dark on the positive print. To a degree, other colors that have a red component also are rendered darker than natural.

Panchromatic film is sensitive to the entire visible spectrum. Its disadvantage is the need to handle it in total darkness for processing. The big advantage to panchromatic film is the natural way it renders shades of color in terms of blacks, grays, and whites.

Yet another factor enters the picture: filtration. Color filters placed in front of the camera lens alter the way black-and-white films record images. Even with panchromatic film, the use of a yellow filter will render blue skies darker than they would appear with no filter.

The task of sorting out colors in black-and-white prints has intrigued aviation historian and author Peter M. Bowers. These shades are described in the book *United States Military Air-*

Million $ Baby *color Kodachrome was obtained after detailed analysis of various black-and-white photos yielded probable color scheme for this Libera-* tor, which was number 44-50768 of the 43rd BG. See text to determine how accurate the reading of the black-and-white photos was. Jeff Ethell Collection

*Photo 1 of* Million $ Baby *shows tones typical of panchromatic film. See chapter text for complete analysis of the col-* or information these black-and-white photos impart. Al Lomer Collection

*craft since 1908*, authored by Bowers and Gordon Swanborough. Bowers and Swanborough say orthochromatic film renders reds dark, yellows quite dark, and blues fairly light. With the advent of panchromatic film, reds were lightened, blues darkened, and yellows could almost appear white, especially if the popular yellow K2 filter was used to snap up the sky definition.

Dana Bell's book *Air Force Colors, Volume I, 1926–1942* asserts that light blue appears so dark when photographed on panchromatic film that it may resemble olive drab.

Let's apply what we know of film characteristics and aircraft markings to the accompanying three photographs of a B-24 Liberator nicknamed *Million $ Baby*, photographed on Ie-Shima in the Pacific in 1945. The photos are so remarkably different in the way they represent the colors of the bathing suit that one might assume the plane had been repainted. But the truth probably lies in the realm of pan and ortho films, and filters.

Photo 1 probably was made with panchromatic film. A clue is the medium shade of the fire extinguisher hatch, located immediately above the woman's raised knee. This hatch was painted red at the factory, providing one reliable color reference as an anchor for further research. The line curving down from her lowest sandal is a snubber mark for towing, to serve as a guide for the maximum turning angle of the nosewheel. It typically was painted black. Expect the antiglare panel on top of the fuselage to be olive drab.

Notice how the red fire extinguisher hatch appears much darker in Photo 2 and 3. This is a clue that they were shot on orthochromatic film. It is logical to expect the woman's painted lips to be red. And they appear the same shade as the red fire extinguisher hatch in all three photos. Similarly, one might suppose the large bow around the woman's neck is red with black shading. Note how the bow is a light shade in the first photo, where it matches the red fire hatch, and the bow is darker in the second and third, where it still matches the red fire extinguisher hatch, which also is rendered darker in appearance.

The panel behind the *Million $ Baby* lettering also seems to mimic the shade of the fire extinguisher hatch, and may also be red. Since orthochromatic film makes little distinction between red and black, the shadow shading on the lettering is obscured in both Photo 2 and 3, if indeed they are orthochromatic, and the panel is red.

The woman's hair color matches the basic shade of her bathing suit in all three photos, turning darker in the second and third. In the panchromatic Photo 1, the hair and bathing suit are light. All these clues indicate the hair and suit are yellow. (Even if the suit looks dark in Photo 3! That's the magic of orthochromatic film.)

The floral designs on the bathing suit may be blue since they appear lighter on the ortho prints (Photo 2 and 3) than on the panchromatic print (Photo 1). Similarly, the large sun hat appears to retain the same tone value as the floral pattern; the hat, too, may be blue.

The sandals change hue in the photos, and are not the same as the hat or swimsuit colors. The sandals are darker in the orthochromatic prints and lighter in the panchromatic print. This might mean they are brown with a high red pigment content. (In the panchromatic Photo 1, the sandals do not have exactly the same tonal value as the fire extinguisher panel, which probably rules out true red for the sandals.)

In the first and second photos, the aircraft data block stenciling can be seen in part of the letter N and the dollar sign. This indicates the lettering was left unpainted, to allow the natural aluminum finish of the B-24 to add shine to the name. The serial appears to be 44-50260; the identifiers FO visible in the original photo in the dollar sign confirm this is a Ford-built Liberator, which matches that s/n. The serial was assigned to a B-24M built at Willow Run, Michigan.

Sleuthing with these three photos has produced a likely composite of the color scheme of this elaborate artwork:

Red: Lips, bow, and sign background

Yellow: Swimsuit and hair

Blue: Floral design on swimsuit and hat

Brown: Sandals

*Photo 2 of* Million $ Baby *renders some shades, like the red fire extinguisher hatch, dark. This suggests it was made* *with orthochromatic film.* Tom Foote Collection

*Photo 3 of* Million $ Baby *could also be from orthochromatic film, with differ-* *ent filtration than Photo 2.* Al Lomer Collection

Flesh tone: Skin

Black: Shadow detailing and outlines

Natural aluminum: Lettering

(Note: This analysis was made with only black-and-white photography to evaluate. Subsequently, a color photo was obtained, and is published in this volume. Refer to it to check the validity of this tonal evaluation.)

The Squaw *was a D-model of the 98th BG that survived the August 1, 1943, low-level Ploesti mission. It was photographed on a promotional tour at Fort Worth, Texas, in 1943. Some patched bullet holes appear to have been painted pale blue and others yellow, in color photos of* The Squaw. *Group emblem and map of the plane's mission history were painted on opposite side of forward fuselage. US Air Force*

*Desert-sand B-24D displays national insignia on both wings, with yellow surrounds and RAF-style fin flashes on both sides of vertical fins. Exhaust has started to smudge the wing behind the engines. Style of individual plane number 84 on tail and nose suggests this Liberator flew with the 376th BG. Gerry Furney Collection*

*The 397th BS in Panama used the considerable talents of PFC William M. Carter to adorn many LB-30s and B-24s with artwork like that on Jungle Queen (AL-640). Jungle Queen served the 6th BG until November 1, 1943, when the group was disbanded; the Panama Liberator squadrons then came under 6th Bomber Command. Jungle Queen was adorned on both sides of the cockpit, with the pose reversed. Data block stenciled beneath cockpit on left side reads: U.S. ARMY LB-30 AC NO. AL-640. Ted Small Collection*

*The Stud Duck adorned 397th BS LB-30 AL-634.* Ted Small Collection

Tiger Lady, *a 6th BG (later, VI Bomber Command) LB-30 that carried number AL641, according to the records of pilot Ted Small. White underbelly blended with wing undersurface, and dropped* *down ahead and behind wing. Similar rise in white can be expected at horizontal tail.* Ted Small Collection

Princess Sheila *was 6th BG LB-30 number AL-639, according to Panama veteran Ted Small.*

Lettie Jo, *another 6th BG LB-30, carried number AL-632.* Ted Small Collection

Peace Offering *may be B-24M-10-FO number 44-50811 of the 529th BS of the 380th BG in the Pacific.* C. M. Young Collection

Bull O' The Woods *bears evidence of an earlier painted-out name—possibly Diablo. According to 397th BS pilot Ted Small's records, this aircraft was LB-30 number AL-583 in service over Panama.* Ted Small Collection

Blonde Blitz *was 6th BG LB-30 number AL-628.* Ted Small Collection

Miss Anabelle Lee *was a B-24 assigned to the 397th BS, in Panama. The last* *three digits of its s/n probably were 957.* Ted Small Collection

Rose O'Day's Daughter *was a B-24 assigned to the 6th BG in Panama, and decorated on both sides. Last three digits of s/n probably were 961.* Ted Small Collection

Night Mission *artwork appeared, in mirror image, on both sides of the fuselage of this 6th BG B-24D, number 42-40891. One panel of this artwork was* *cut from the bomber as it was scrapped, and is preserved by the Confederate Air Force.* Ted Small and Peter M. Bowers Collections

Bail-out Belle *was a B-24D (s/n 42-72951), probably assigned to the 529th BS of the 380th BG in the Pacific. The art appeared in mirror image on both sides of nose, and remained after the plane's camouflage paint was stripped to bare metal. When a Hawaii Air Depot nose turret was added, the .50cal cheek gun port was skinned over. A machine gun ball socket was installed in the navigator's window. Lee Bushnell and Larry Jaynes Collections*

Some color deterioration cannot hide the beauty of Lucky Strike, *which may be B-24M-5-CO 44-41876 of the 530th Squadron of the 380th BG in 1945. C. M. Young Collection*

Sure Pop *was B-24D-CO-130 s/n 42-41073, assigned to the 90th BG, and probably the 319th BS. Extreme discoloration shows where nose-turret addition caused new olive paint to be added over its faded coat. Larry Jaynes Collection*

Gus' Jokers *was the last B-24M-1-CO (44-41848), and flew with the 31st BS of the 5th BG. Dark background with last three digits of s/n in white on forward fuselages of 5th BG B-24s gave way in 1945 to the last four digits being painted directly on the aluminum sides of the forward fuselages. C. E. Larsson and Albert W. James Collections*

Booby Trap *carried the smiling skull of the Fifth AF's 90th BG on Pacific missions. Its s/n may be 44-40193. Dennis Peltier and Larry Jaynes Collections*

C-87 *number 44-39229 in the CBI showed a replacement cargo door with a piece of national insignia differently placed than on the rest of the plane. Oily exhaust smudged the lower curve of the vertical fin. This photo is one of many taken under crude field conditions by aviation historian Peter M. Bowers, who, as an AAF officer, used discarded aerial film that he trimmed in the darkroom to fit 616 size film spools when his limited supply of film ran out. Peter M. Bowers Collection*

*An unnamed bulldog adorned a British Liberator in India.*

V Grand, *the 5,000th Convair San Diego B-24, was autographed by Consolidated Vultee workers before going off to war with the Fifteenth AF. This B-24J-195-CO twice made emergency landings on the island of Vis, in the Adriatic Sea, between Italy and Yugoslavia. She probably served with the 454th BG. In service,* V Grand *received Fifteenth AF-style enclosed waist windows with K-5 gun mounts, but retained the wind deflectors. General Dynamics, Herb Tollefson, and Charlie Glassie Collections*

Pistol Packin' Mama, *one of the most popular of all B-24 nose art names, adorned this Fifteenth AF example in Italy. Additional windows have been added in the nose; wavy camouflage demarcation suggests this is a Ford-built Liberator.* Charlie Glassie Collection

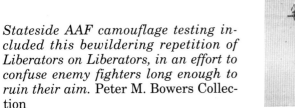

*Stateside AAF camouflage testing included this bewildering repetition of Liberators on Liberators, in an effort to confuse enemy fighters long enough to ruin their aim.* Peter M. Bowers Collection

*A scaly, grinning creature adorned this Eighth AF B-24, which had add-on cockpit armor glass. The Emerson A-15 nose turret is an early model with front Plexiglas extending all the way to the bottom of the turret.* Al Lloyd Collection

## Chapter 6

# Join the Navy

## Protecting the Sea Lanes

Antisubmarine missions often were characterized by long hours of tedious overwater flying, where great range and reasonable speed were desirable traits in an aircraft. The US Navy found range, if not speed, in its strut-braced PBY Catalina seaplanes and amphibians.

But the province of heavy bombardment airplanes remained with the Army Air Corps. The slick new Davis wing, tried by Consolidated first on the experimental Model 31 flying boat for the Navy, found a home on the Army's Model 32 Liberator. When the Air Corps gained acceptance for heavy bombers in the 1930s, the idealized mission involved flying out to sea to meet enemy ships, and sinking them before they could attack the United States. In the minds of AAF planners, land-based heavy bombers as antisubmarine weapons were logically the AAF's obligation and turf. American policy limited the Navy's use of land-based planes. Inroads in this provincial plan were made with amphibious PBY-5A Catalinas, and with Lockheed Hudson twin-engine land-based bombers requisitioned by the Navy in October 1941. The Navy got into the land-based

*An early greenhouse PB4Y-1 over England, 1943.* National Archives

bomber business with the Hudsons plausibly because the use of seaplanes for America's Neutrality Patrol from Newfoundland and Iceland was threatened by winter icing conditions on the water. George F. Poulos, who served as operations officer and executive officer of Navy PB4Y-1 squadron VB-103, was well acquainted with the early politics involved in antisubmarine duties. Writing in the Spring 1991 *Briefing* of the International B-24 Liberator Club, Poulos recalled that Gen. George C. Marshall proposed a Coastal Air Command for the AAF, to have domain over Liberators and other landplanes in maritime usage, when the Navy urged development of naval antisubmarine squadrons of landplanes. "This disagreement was consistent with the basic differences that existed between the Navy and the Army organizational concepts," Poulos said. "The Navy believed that the *function* was the primary basis for organization, whereas the Army operated on the theory that the *weapon* should be the prime organizational consideration." In other words, the AAF figured if the mission demanded a Liberator, an AAF crew would fly it. But the Navy believed if a largely maritime mission required a special landplane, that landplane should be given to the Navy to do the job right.

Perhaps it was the breakthrough in range and speed of the Liberator itself that encouraged the Navy to rethink

its classic reliance on waterborne patrol bombers, and pursue faster landplanes. The trackless ocean could be monitored with long-legged, land-based Liberators. In the early months of American combat in 1942, the faster speed of aerodynamically streamlined land-based patrol bombers paid dividends when the Navy's PBO-1 Hudsons sank two U-boats because the Hudsons could close to attacking range faster than the lumbering Catalinas. The Catalinas could be seen on the horizon by surfaced submariners, who had more time to crash-dive than they did with the Hudsons on the prowl. Other problems dogged the seaplanes, particularly when engaged by enemy fighters, during which the survivability of a slow seaplane was considered less than that of a faster landplane bomber.

As early as February 1942, the Navy asked for a share of B-24 production deliveries to bolster naval antisub patrols. But the AAF was not easily persuaded to give up that mission—or a portion of its B-24 Liberator heavy bombers—in the struggling months of the first year of war. The Navy had an asset coveted by the AAF: The Boeing factory on the south shore of Lake Washington, at Renton, Washington, was earmarked for production of PBB-1 Sea Ranger patrol seaplanes. This plant was ideal for construction of the new B-29 Superfortress for the AAF. Even while arrayed against the com-

*Wing-mounted radar antennas aided this early US Navy PB4Y-1 in finding ships and surfaced submarines.* Peter M. Bowers Collection

mon Axis enemy abroad, the Navy and AAF bartered shrewdly with one another at home. Chief of Staff George C. Marshall agreed, on July 7, 1942, to cleave off part of Consolidated's Liberator production to meet Navy needs. The Navy also was given a share of Mitchell and Ventura production. The AAF was pleased to get the Boeing Renton plant when the Navy declared the Sea Ranger moot, thereby freeing up shop space and R-3350 engines for the B-29 assembly line to be created there. To further enhance production of the Liberators the Navy and AAF both wanted, the Navy agreed to limit its orders for Catalinas, also built by Consolidated in San Diego, to minimize interference with Liberator production.

The Navy had its own nomenclature for aircraft during World War II. All Navy Liberators were built as PB4Y-1s, whether delivered with a B-24D greenhouse nose, the Navy's ERCO bow turret, or, in some instances, the Emerson nose. All Privateers were delivered as PB4Y-2s. (Some acquired the designator PB4Y-2B to indicate they were fitted for slinging Bat glide bombs under their wings.) By 1962, the American services adopted a universal nomenclature for aircraft by which the few remaining Privateers in Navy service were redesignated basically P-4, and more narrowly, QP-4B, as drone aircraft.

By August 1942, Navy PB4Y-1 Liberators were reality. On November 5, 1942, the first Navy Liberator to sink a U-boat recorded this feat while operating out of Iceland.

A year would pass, in which the AAF also flew B-24Ds on antisubmarine patrols. Not until August 1943 did the AAF agree to disband its own Anti-

submarine Command, putting this specialized mission squarely in the hands of the Navy. The AAF antisubmarine squadrons would phase out gradually as the Navy was able to replace them. According to George Poulos' account, the AAF's 479th Antisubmarine Group's 19th Squadron departed Dunkeswell, England, on September 7, 1943, to join up with the Eighth AF. The AAF's 6th Squadron left Dunkeswell on September 22, and two days later, Navy squadron VB-103 moved to Dunkeswell from St. Eval. The Army's 22nd Squadron departed St. Eval on September 28, but the AAF's 4th Squadron continued to patrol the Bay of Biscay until October 31, 1943. By then, a third Navy Liberator squadron was ready to join 103 and 105 squadrons, according to Poulos.

Some swapouts of bombers occurred, as the Navy inherited radar-equipped antisubmarine Liberators from the AAF in place of some of the Navy's early PB4Y-1s, which lacked

To comply with aspects of Portuguese neutrality so they could use the Azores during World War II, some VB-114 PB4Y-1s curiously carried dual US and British markings. This example, BuNo. 32205, carried a Leigh searchlight under its right wing. Propeller hubs and blades out to the diameter of the cowling sometimes were painted white to blend with the nacelles. Donald C. Higgins via Liberator Club Collection

Not all nose-turret PB4Y-1s used ER-CO bow turrets; some, like PB4Y-1 BuNo. 38894, flew with AAF-style Emerson nose turrets instead. This aircraft came from the second-to-last batch of San Diego B-24Js, and carried Navy tri-color camouflage. Peter M. Bowers Collection

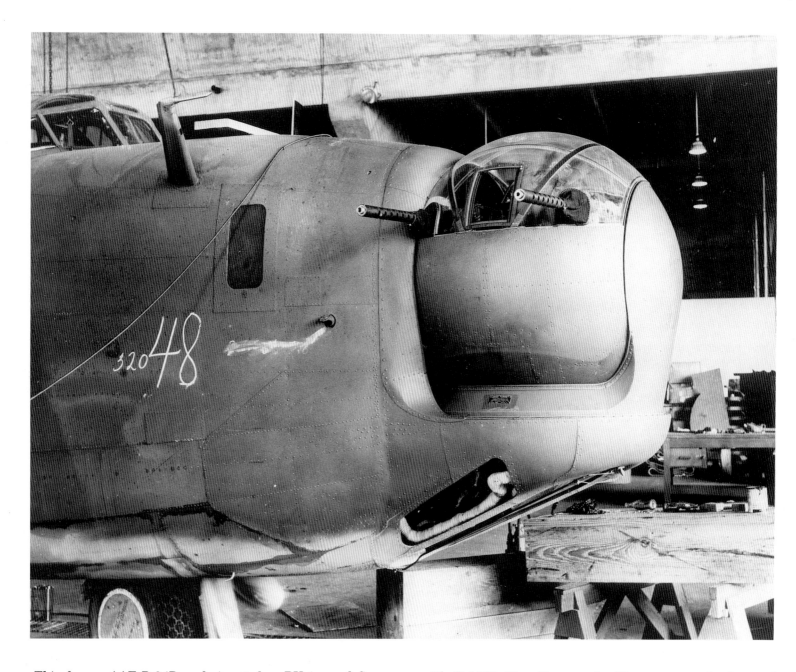

*This former AAF B-24D, redesignated PB4Y-1 number 32048, received an ER-CO bow turret installation at North Island Naval Air Station in May 1943.* Chuck Hansen Collection

the electronics needed to find subs beyond visual range.

Typically, Navy PB4Y-1 Liberators were built by Consolidated in San Diego; when single-tail Privateers were introduced, all of these sophisticated PB4Y-2s were San Diego products.

During World War II, the Navy dabbled in transport Liberators, flying three C-87s with R-1830-45 engines as

RY-1s, and five more with R-1830-43 powerplants. A transport version of the Privateer, designated RY-3, flew briefly with the Navy and Marines, but slipped out of service quietly in post-war years. Fewer than 40 RY-3s were built for the Navy and Marines; some saw service with the RAF.

### Navy Nose Jobs

The Navy soon acknowledged the need for improved frontal firepower in its PB4Y-1s, and grafted ERCO (Engineering and Research Corp.) spherical turrets to some of its greenhouse PB4Y-1s. These were the same bow turrets designed for the PBB-1 Sea

Ranger the Navy gave up in favor of getting a share of landplane production runs. A test contract for equipping a combat squadron of PB4Y-1s with ER-CO bow turrets was let in the summer of 1942, as the Navy wasted no time in upgrading its Liberators. Results were favorable, and combat losses of ERCO-equipped Liberators were said to diminish.

After removing the greenhouse, a protruding lip containing the turret ring was mounted and faired into the fuselage contours. Shallow quarters for the bombardier below the large turret included a large, flat optical aiming window, usually bracketed by two small scanning windows. Later PB4Y-1s and PB4Y-2 Privateers used larger, more effective scanning windows.

The ERCO Model 250SH bow turret had an upper surface of Plexiglas held in place by metal straps; the clear portion could be removed for emergency escape. The two .50cal machine guns in the turret were rigidly mounted; the entire ball, encasing the gunner, was moved by hydraulic pressure in azimuth and elevation to track targets. The door to the turret served as a padded backrest for the gunner. Spent shells and links were collected internally, with links falling into zippered canvas bags beneath each gun, while the empty brass gathered in an internal compartment in the lower front of the turret, accessible from the outside following a mission.

Some Navy records indicate some PB4Y-1s and later PB4Y-2 Privateers were ferried, minus ERCO bow turrets, from the Consolidated San Diego factory to nearby North Island Naval Air Station, also in San Diego, for the turret installation. Photos accompanying this text show an early PB4Y-1 receiving its ERCO turret at North Island. However, a footnote in the PB4Y-2 Privateer parts catalog says: "Airplanes 59433 to 66324 inclusive furnished with dummy nose fairing forward of station 9.1 and instal[lation] of nose-turret structure and turret accomplished at Litchfield Park [Arizona] as a Navy modification." This series of Privateers, starting with BuNo. 59433, may correspond with those Privateers receiving ERCO bow turrets. Photos of Privateers with Consolidated/MPC-style nose turrets generally depict aircraft with lower BuAer numbers. The basic aircraft manufacturers were constantly playing catch-up with modifications. Sometimes, to keep production moving at an even pace, it was simpler to complete an aircraft with a known deficiency, and send it immediately to a modification center for update, than it was to create turmoil in the basic assembly process by trying to insert all the newest changes at the factory.

## Navy Combat

The November 1942 sinking of a U-boat was followed by years of diligent combat flown by Navy and Marine aviators in PB4Ys. War and weather were

*During a Bay of Biscay patrol, US Navy PB4Y-1 pilot Charles F. Willis, Jr., buzzed a downed example of his German equivalent, a cracked-up Focke-Wulf Fw 200, somewhere in Spain.* Charles F. Willis, Jr., Collection

*In the January chill of 1944, Charlie Willis' PB4Y-1 found and sank this German submarine from an altitude of 100ft.* Charles F. Willis, Jr., Collection

Blue Belle *flew photo recon for Navy squadron VD-5 when this photo was taken on Iwo Jima early in 1945.* San Diego Aerospace Museum

quick, unforgiving teachers to the new Navy crews, some of whom were veterans of Pacific Catalina combat. VB-103 launched Liberators from Argentia, Newfoundland, beginning in May 1943, escorting convoys to mid-Atlantic. Veteran George Poulos recalled: "On June 23, while en route to rendezvous with a convoy, Lt. H. K. Reese reported a radar blip and came through a very heavy overcast to investigate. No further messages were received. My search of the area the next day, in perfect weather, uncovered three huge icebergs. We all learned from this incident and . . . when investigating an isolated radar blip in bad weather we always allowed a five degree offset on the radar scope until we had visual contact."

As a footnote to the history of the Vought F4U Corsair fighter, it was while escorting PB4Y-1 Liberators of squadron VP-51 on a daylight shipping strike over Kahili, Bougainville, that the gull-wing Corsair first saw air-to-air combat on February 13, 1943.

The summer of 1943 did not pay out in submarine contacts for the crews of VB-103. Evidently the escort carriers were being so successful that the U-boats were prompted to haunt different waters. On August 15, 1943, VB-103 departed Argentia for St. Eval, England, arriving two days later. AAF antisubmarine B-24D squadrons at Gander also departed for England during this time.

Over the North Atlantic and the Bay of Biscay, Navy Liberators in distinctive white-bottomed, high-sided camouflage did their best to scrub the cold sea clean of German submarines. PB4Y-1s occasionally asserted themselves in unlikely air-to-air combat against their four-engine Luftwaffe counterpart, the FW 200 Kondor. During the summer of 1943, the Luftwaffe began launching twin-engine fighter variants of the Ju 88 to seek out Allied patrol planes like the PB4Y-1s. To this threat, the British responded effectively with sweeps by Bristol Beaufighters and deHavilland Mosquitoes.

On occasion, PB4Y-1 crews out of England were engaged by Messerschmitt Bf 109 fighters. The big Davis wing, skillfully flown, could foil the attacks of a lone Messerschmitt by turning the fighter's higher wing loading

against it in tight maneuvering. If the Luftwaffe pilot attempted to follow the Liberator into the turn, the fighter risked a stall. At low altitude over the icy waves, such a stall could prove fatal to the fighter. This gave the Bf 109 pilot a dilemma, for if he broke off the turn, he lost his shot at the Liberator. If the lone PB4Y-1s of the Navy lacked the umbrella of combined firepower that their AAF counterparts enjoyed in mass formations, the solo Navy bombers at least had the freedom to maneuver in the open sky to shake off their attacker.

The Marines took greenhouse PB4Y-1s into Pacific combat with squadron VMD-254. Some of their Liberators packed a fixed cannon in the nose—Marines aren't shy about using firepower in combat.

It was the fall doldrums when Navy squadron VPB-108 came to the Pacific in 1943, to fly in the campaign to take the Gilbert Islands. Beginning November 17, the Liberator crews of VPB-108 mocked weather that grounded other planes. They soon began exercising their Yankee ingenuity. They flew their PB4Y-1s on the deck, downwind, at top speed, and under radar detection height and then popped up to 150ft to drop bombs by eyeball. Lt. Frank W. Ackermann in *Pistol Packin' Mama* tried the trick out, against Mille, in the Marshall Islands. Strafing down one side of the island, Ackermann circled the harbor and claimed a supply ship sunk by two bombs. Squadron accounts say he flew 15ft above the Mille runway, as his gunners strafed everything of value. Six Japanese fighters engaged his Liberator—two went down, one was damaged, and the rest failed to bring Ackermann down. Lt. Richard B. Daley repeated the trick three days later, flying *Nippo Nippin' Kitten* to Jaluit Atoll. Among targets Daley's crew claimed that day were two fuel storage tanks, a landing barge filled with troops, and a Kawanishi H8K Emily flying boat, resting on the water. The pace was set. The squadron moved in about a month to position themselves for the battle of the Marshall Islands.

In January 1944, Lt. Comdr. Edward Renfro, skipper of VPB-108, led 10 Liberators on a palm-shaking run over Kwajalein. The surprise element

was so effective only one enemy gunner fired back on the first pass, only to be silenced by a gunner in a PB4Y-1. The bold attack inflicted damage on the Japanese garrison—and was staged as a diversion to permit two camera planes access to low-oblique photography of Kwajalein useful in subsequent major attacks.

Two VPB-108 Liberators hung in the air 19hr to reach Wake Island, and return, on February 28, 1944. They dropped 500lb bombs from less than 100ft.

Relieved at Eniwetok by VPB-116 on July 10, 1944, VPB-108 was reformed on September 20 that same year at Alameda, California, this time with new PB4Y-2 Privateers.

The first bombing mission against Iwo Jima by landplanes was a July 14, 1944, strike by Navy PB4Y-1 Liberators of VB-109, flying out of Saipan. The distinctions between AAF and Navy targets, and aircraft, were blurring as the dictates of combat set the pace.

In October 1944, the Navy revised its nomenclature for bombing squadrons. Multi-engine bombing squadrons that had been signified by *VB* combined their terminology with patrol squadrons, that had been *VP,* to form the single designation *VPB,* used for the remainder of the war.

On May 13, 1945, the Navy put up what was to have been a mixed three-plane formation of two PB4Y-1s and

*Ranging out from Whidbey Island Naval Air Station in Washington state, Privateer 59604 sported mottled paint scheme applied to some PB4Y-2s. View shows paired antennas under nose for scanning either side of plane's line of flight.*

one single-tail PB4Y-2, loaded with incendiaries for the destruction of the Pontianak, Borneo, shipyard, according to mission participant R. L. Wolpert. The performance advantage of the Privateer prompted its crew to bomb early, leaving a fire licking at the shipyard when the two PB4Y-1 Liberators of VPB-111 arrived on scene. Wolpert, copilot on one of the Liberators, noted

in on him simultaneously and a head-on collision was averted only by what I have always believed was a miracle."

## Tall Tail

With the Navy's foot squarely in the door of Liberator production, it is not surprising a Navy-encouraged derivative of the Liberator took form on Consolidated drawing boards. Many ingredients combined in this process: Consolidated already had in mind field-of-fire improvements for Liberator gunners that a single tail could provide. Independent of Navy studies, the AAF and Consolidated pieced together the B-24ST (Single Tail) and XB-24K (essentially one program using spliced airframes and a tall tail from a B-23 Dragon bomber). The AAF test plane began flying in March 1943; the Navy ordered three prototype single-tail variants of its own on May 3 of that same year.

Both the AAF and Navy variants enjoyed benefits of improved stability and handling from the single-tail configurations. But the route to Privateer production was not the same path the AAF followed in its single-tail Liberator projects. The Navy wanted a long-range radar search plane. To house the secret electronics suite of the Privateer, a fuselage extension of seven feet was spliced into the three prototypes ahead of the wings, as PB4Y-1s numbers 32095, 32096, and 32086 were dissected to become the first Privateers.

The basic Privateer form was comparison-tested with a standard greenhouse PB4Y-1 model in the University of Washington wind tunnel. Configuration changes included tests with the large ventral radome (located in the new fuselage plug) extended for operation, and with bulging side gun blisters, evoking images of "form follows function" engineering. The single tail of the model was an early version; on production Privateers, it was heightened still more. The wind-tunnel model was also tested in a hybrid form—lengthened and studded with protuberances like a Privateer, but retaining the twin tails of a Liberator.

Consolidated's San Diego plant delivered all three XPB4Y-2 prototypes with twin tails, even though the single tail was an integral part of the plan. The lengthened bombers flew first in

*Privateer* Tortilla Flat *served in VPB-106, surviving combat before returning to Camp Kearney, near San Diego, for training use. Sharkmouth appears to have "gums" in red, and pinstriped outer lips and spaces between teeth in black.* David Behunin and John Dingle Collections

his plane received a few hits from the alerted enemy. A lone Mitsubishi Ki-51 Sonia, packing two wing-mounted machine guns and probably equipped with a flexible machine gun in the rear cockpit, gamely attacked the two Liberators. No doubt to the surprise of the Japanese pilot, the Liberators returned the attack, as Wolpert's pilot peeled off and went after the Sonia in a banking shallow dive! The dogfight might have looked arthritic compared to a full-blown duel between front-line fighters, but the slow Sonia and the big PB4Y-1s slugged it out for about a half hour, Wolpert recalled in the Fall 1989 *Briefing* of the International B-24 Liberator Club. "It was only because there were two of us and one of him that we finally got that Sonia," Wolpert said. "Fact is, at one point near the end, he damned near got both of us. We had him at the apex of a loose 'V' formation when he performed a perfect Immelman and came back between us. We were so intent on our target that we both turned

September, October, and December 1943 as they were sent to the Navy. Later that year, all three returned to San Diego for Consolidated's installation of the original short single tail. The Navy took the revised XPB4Y-2s again on February 2, 1944. The first two prototypes kept standard B-24 engine nacelle packages; the third prototype introduced the vertical oval shape, minus turbo-superchargers, that would characterize production Privateers.

The first version of the single tail was inadequate. After examining some expedient fixes proposed by Consolidated designers, the Navy decided the best answer involved new engineering for a still taller tail, to top out at a stunning 29ft, 1-5/8in above the tarmac.

The tail increase delayed deliveries of Privateers, but resulted in a better airplane, generally liked by crews.

The three XPB4Y-2 prototypes carried Consolidated nose turrets, replaced on early production Privateers by similar MPC turrets that made the noses of the first Privateers look strikingly like a contemporary B-24 Liberator. The definitive Privateer nose was the ERCO bow turret installation as applied to later Navy PB4Y-1s.

## Equipping the Privateer

The Norden bombsight, so central to AAF strategic bombardment, found little favor with the Navy, since antishipping strikes were more successful at low altitudes, where the Norden's abilities waned. According to a document produced by Navy historian Lee Pearson in 1974, "Up until early 1944, the Norden sight was installed in all new patrol planes and torpedo bombers. . . . Regulations also required that bombsights be in the aircraft whenever they were transferred. Deemphasis of the Norden sight began early in 1944 when the requirement that it be transferred with the aircraft was dropped. In February and March of 1945, the requirement for its installation was also cancelled." Nonetheless, Navy bombers including Privateers sometimes retained the stabilizer portion of the Norden bombsight equipment, which could be used as an autopilot or to stabilize a Privateer for radar bombing.

Some Privateer pilots used visual cues at low altitude, and bombed without bombsights, and in some cases, without a bombardier aboard.

Though enemy submarines gave impetus to the Navy's original desire

Miss Sea-duce *followed a common Pacific practice of allowing nose art to encroach on plane numbers.* Jim Masura Collection

for Liberators, by the time Privateers left the United States for Pacific action, the probability of encountering a friendly submarine largely precluded

*Sailing low over a wood-paneled station wagon is a PB4Y-2 at Whidbey Island Naval Air Station, Washington.*

*Privateer 59640 was photographed in September 1946 with JATO (jet-assisted takeoff) bottles attached on the fuselage ahead of and behind the bomb bays.* Warren Bodie via Peter M. Bowers Collection

antisubmarine missions in Privateers. D. A. Rosso, Jr., who served as a radio-radar-countermeasures aircrewman on Privateers in VPB-124, told historian Pearson: "We did not do ASW [antisubmarine warfare] per se. If a sub was on the surface, we would treat it as any other surface target." Rosso recalled that his Privateer did not have mag-

netic-anomaly-detection (MAD) gear, or sonobuoys, to aid in finding submerged submarines.

Rosso recalled using ASG radar—referred to as George gear—(and probably superceded by AN/APS-2 equipment) for searches: "I can remember getting landfalls on Okinawa at 90 to 100mi consistently when returning from missions."

A Navy airborne radar countermeasures manual covering World War II applications glibly says: "The designers of RCM [radar countermeasures] installations in naval aircraft have made an effort to provide a lay-out which will help you operate the equip-

ment with the maximum comfort and to produce the maximum inconvenience to the enemy." RCM components were designed in standard module sizes of about 10in wide by 8in high and 22in deep, or in half-size cases that were only 5in wide. This facilitated swapping out RCM components to change the suite to meet differing tactical situations.

The Navy manual describes a typical PB4Y-2 radar installation: "RCM search installations are somewhat more elaborate on the large patrol planes. Typical of these is the PB4Y-2 which carries a direction finder and a microwave search receiver, in addition to the usual AN/APR-1 receiver and AN/APA-11 pulse analyzer." Additionally, Privateers carried a selection from the following RCM equipment allowance for the PB4Y-2:

AN/APR-1 search receiver
AN/APR-2 recording search receiver
AN/APR-5A microwave search receiver
AN/ARR-5 communications search receiver
AN/ARR-7 communications search receiver
AN/APA-10 panoramic adaptor
AN/APA-11 pulse analyzer
AN/APA-17 direction finder (high frequency)
AN/APA-24 direction finder (low frequency)
AN/APA-23 recorder attachment
AN/APA-3S panoramic adaptor
AN/APT-1 jamming transmitter
AN/APQ-2 jamming transmitter
AN/APT-5 jamming transmitter

The antenna array under the nose of a Privateer typically included four pairs of antennas for search and jamming. Each pair was located to scan opposite sides of the Privateer's path; hence a similar row of antenna bumps occurred on the left and right (port and starboard) sides of the lower nose. The array included: AS-124/APR, for receiving signals between 300 and 1,000 megacycles; the AS-67/APQ-2B, for use with the AN/APQ-2 transmitter listed above; the AS-125/APR, for use with the AN/APR-5 receiver for signals in the 1,000–3,000 megacycle range; and the AT-53/AP, for receiving signals between 100 and 300 megacycles.

Since each side of the nose antenna array covered only that side of the Privateer's flight, the RCM manual instructed: "It is necessary to switch from side to side when searching an area in which signals may come from any direction." An antenna switch was provided the operator, the manual said, so that "a flip of the wrist will connect the search receiver to any desired antenna or direction finder." Coaxial cables ran from each antenna to a patchboard, where short jumper cables were used to connect the most-used antennas to the antenna selector switch for the needs of a particular mission. For receiving signals below 100 megacycles,

the PB4Y-2 was equipped with AT-54/AP stubs that could be switched with the AT-53 or AT-52 stub antennas that can often be seen behind the four paired antenna bumps.

*PB4Y-2 Privateer V521 shared ramp space with several other Navy patrol planes.* Jeff Ethell Collection

### Privateer Combat

VPB-106 took a dozen new PB4Y-2 Privateers through Hawaii and out into the Pacific for combat, leaving late in 1944. They flew a mixed group of bombers, some with the early MPC nose turret, and some with the later standard ERCO bow unit. The squadron lost one Privateer to Japanese fighters over Singapore. There was nothing the second PB4Y-2 in the two-plane formation could do as fire burned through the right wing, sending the stricken bomber inverted into the sea. Three other PB4Y-2s of VPB-106 simply failed to return from patrol.

VPB-108, champions of low-level Liberator attacks in the central Pacific, returned to the fray on April 4, 1945, in PB4Y-2 Privateers. That day, Lt. Comdr. Robert C. Lefever made a glide-bombing and strafing attack on antiaircraft positions at West Ngatpang. The Privateers of VPB-108 based out of Peleliu, and then Tinian and Iwo Jima. Early in May 1945, three of 108's Privateers joined six planes from VPB-102 in a strike on Marcus intended to thwart rumored Japanese attacks staging through there, to hit the American

anchorage at Ulithi. Three of the VPB-102 bombers arrived first, and when the three Privateers of VPB-108 roared in, Japanese defenses were primed. Lieutenant Commander Muldrow and crew went down in a Privateer shedding pieces, and one complete engine, before crashing into the sea. Somehow, five men survived, and were rescued by the US Navy. Muldrow was not among the fortunate.

A closing act for Privateers of VPB-102, 108, 109, 116, and 121 was flying barrier patrols to keep Japanese recon planes and kamikazes from damaging the Third Fleet as it sailed nearer to Japan.

On August 11, 1945, after two atom bombs convinced the Japanese to seek peace, but scant days before a ceasefire, two Privateers of VPB-121, flown by Lt. Comdrs. J. B. Rainey and T. G. Allen, cruised near the coastline of Honshu, south of Tokyo and Yokohama. Nearing the end of their mission and about to turn for base, the two Privateers were bounced by a half-dozen Japanese fighters. Even with the Privateers' impressive firepower, Rainey's blue bomber was downed in a matter of

*Characteristic Privateer cowling used cooling inlets of different sizes on top and bottom, instead of the side-to-side symmetry of the B-24/PB4Y-1. Frederick A. Johnsen*

*Bearing modified cockpit and B-25 engine packages as used on Super Privateer civilian fire bomber conversions, the US Naval Aviation Museum's Privateer looked like this in February 1992, on outdoor display at the museum's Pensacola, Florida, site. This is the first Privateer to enter a museum collection.*

seconds. Allen's P4Y-2 took hits and limped home with a wounded tail gunner. The tragedy occurred on VPB-121's last mission of World War II.

## Chapter 7

# Liberators in Postwar Service

Though an American bomber first and foremost, Liberators served other countries during and after World War II. Most obvious is the use of Liberators, way back to the prewar Liberator I, by the RAF. RAF Liberators included greenhouse D-model equivalents, on through nose-turret models. (The world's current supply of Fort Worth-built B-24Js is attributable to RAF Liberators left behind in India in the late 1940s.)

Along with the RAF, the RCAF, RAAF, and South African Air Force all flew Liberators during World War II.

Turkey impounded a HALPRO B-24D, 41-11596, and ultimately received others before war's end.

Nationalist China acquired B-24s, including some M-models. In the Cold War years, the Nationalist Chinese also operated dark-blue PB4Y-2 Privateers.

The French Navy used some of its PB4Y-2s to bomb Indochina; others served in French colonial North Africa.

In Honduras, Privateers minus armament served the armed forces.

*Tinted red, white, and blue water cascaded from the tanks of Hawkins and Powers Privateer air tanker number 127 during a demonstration at the Reno National Championship Air Races, September 1975. Frederick A. Johnsen*

Most celebrated among the postwar users was the Indian Air Force (IAF). Hindustan Aircraft Industries rebuilt Liberators of various models after the RAF disabled them and abandoned them in country. India flew B-24Js, Ls, and Ms, as well as at least one C-87. The Indian Liberators served as maritime recon aircraft as late as 1968, fitted with turrets also rebuilt in India.

Nazi Germany captured B-24s and tested them for defensive strengths and weaknesses.

**After the War**

The end of World War II quickly put B-24s out of business in the AAF. For bombardment, masses of B-29s were available, with B-36s and jet B-47s on the horizon. For transport, C-54s, C-82s, and bigger purpose-built transports were in the inventory or on the way. For training, proficiency, and utility purposes, there was an almost universal rejection of the B-24 in the postwar Air Force in favor of docile B-17s, or B-25s. The few B-24s remaining in service after V-J Day typically flew tests, either for atmospheric research or as platforms for new radar defenses or jet engine trials.

The US Navy treated its Liberators and Privateers differently. While putting postwar dollars into new carriers and new aircraft for the carriers, the Navy retained Privateers to aug-

ment P2V Neptunes in patrol work. PB4Y-1s continued to serve in Navy photo mapping squadrons well into the 1950s. It may have been economics—the Navy had less access to an abundance of large airframes than did the Air Force, and could ill afford to dispose of all its Liberators and Privateers.

In 1949, VP-61 earned a flying safety award for keeping its six PB4Y-1P (*P* designated Photo) Liberators flying for 5,000hr without an accident. "It is one of the few units in the armed services still using Liberators," noted a story in the March 1949 *Naval Aviation News*. For the two years prior to the award, VP-61 extensively photo-mapped Alaska, including 68,000 square miles of the slope of Alaska, to be used in oil exploration in Naval Petroleum Reserve Number Four. Mosaics taken by the cameras in VP-61's Liberators also enhanced the accuracy of US Geological Survey maps of Alaska. These blue Liberators carried K-17 6in focal-length cameras, K-18 24in focal-length cameras, and Fairchild CA-8 cartographic cameras.

Mapping Kodiak Island in 1947, crews learned they needed to hone their level-flying skills to an incredible degree to afford the cameras the most uniform platform for consistency. Tilting of the wings could throw a photo's accuracy off. During 1948, VP-61 practiced its skills over the Imperial Valley of California before returning to tackle Alaska again. VP-61 was given credit for vital contributions to a federal program of surveying Alaska's resources.

Records kept by the Navy indicate the last squadron use of twin-tail Liberators was with VJ-62, flying P4Y-1P (the *B* was deleted from nomenclature) aircraft on May 31, 1956.

The Navy did not preserve any of its PB4Y-1s. One surplus Navy greenhouse Liberator was flown to Troutdale, Oregon, in the years following World War II. Its intended purpose—becoming a gas station ornament—was accomplished by a different entrepreneur using a new surplus B-17G, so the tri-color blue Navy Liberator was sold to California-Atlantic Airways of St. Petersburg, Florida, eventually winding up in Bolivia, according to Bob Sturges, whose Columbia Airmotive Co. was involved with negotiations on the Liberator.

Navy patrol squadrons continued to fly radar-studded Privateers in the 1950s pending replacement, typically by P2V Neptunes. Postwar Privateer squadrons in the US Navy included VP-22, VP-23, VP-24, VP-25, VJ-2 (called "hurricane hunters"), VP-772, VP-9, and VP-871 (the latter three flying Korean War combat missions).

*Their combats over, Liberators in various Eighth AF group markings awaited scrapping at Albuquerque (Sandia),* New Mexico, in 1946. Don Alberts Collection

### Eye of the Storm

Squadron VP-23 gained fame as hurricane hunters before VJ-2 took the duty in Florida. In 1950, *Naval Aviation News* detailed the procedure VP-23's PB4Y-2s used to breach hurricanes: "The usual procedure is to circumnavigate about 30 miles out from the center with surface winds of 60 knots commencing in the southeastern quadrant." When the Privateer crew estimated their position to be due north of the eye of the storm, as 60 knots of wind beat against the plane, it would penetrate the storm. As the dark blue bomber progressed toward the eye of the spiraling hurricane, dramatic decreases in barometric pressure accompanied increases in wind speed. Depending on how much the Privateer was being tossed by the hurricane, actual entry into the eye of the storm was at the pilot's discretion, according to the published account. Once the eye was picked up on the radar scope, actual penetration was no longer necessary. The eye of the storm could be picked up from 15 to 20mi away, and sometimes as far as 30mi away.

Anytime the storm got too violent, the Privateer could exit by making slow, flat rudder turns to the right, while holding attitude and altitude. The turn to the right for escape was held until the wind "is just abaft the starboard beam, making course adjustments to keep it there until out of

Badger Beauty, *awaiting its fate in a boneyard in Albuquerque, New Mexico, in 1946, showed evidence of a Ford-* style antiglare panel in flat black—not all B-24s had olive green antiglare paint. Don Alberts Collection

This tiger-faced Eighth AF B-24 with red Emerson nose turret spent its final days in a scrapping field at Kirtland Army Airfield, Albuquerque, New Mexico, after World War II. Don Alberts Collection

Turkish markings on the rudders indicate new ownership for this B-24. Faint overpainted patches on vertical stabilizers probably hide RAF-style fin flashes used in the Mediterranean by AAF B-24s in 1942–1943. This aircraft may be Halverson Detachment B-24D 41-11596, nicknamed Brooklyn Rambler, which landed in Turkey after the early Ploesti mission of June 11, 1942. Interned by the Turks, the crew took Brooklyn Rambler back in a bold escape. The Turkish government protested, and the B-24 was given back to Turkey, without the crew, following some repairs that were made to the plane in Eritrea. Herb Tollefson Collection

*British Liberator II modification resembled US LB-30/C-87 conversions, but had distinct round portholes. New-style deicer boots were added by the time of the photo (July 1946).* Peter M. Bowers Collection

*Commando, Winston Churchill's aircraft, was the second Liberator II built (AL504). Consolidated's Tucson, Arizona, modification center altered Commando in 1944 with a single tail, cargo doors, and fuselage extension, creating a virtual RY-3 that retained its original powerplant packages. It is said that Churchill never flew in the modified Commando.* Peter M. Bowers Collection

heavy weather or turbulence," the account related.

## Flare for Korean Combat

Six years after flying solo shipping sorties against the Japanese, PB4Y-2s went to Korea to help thwart communist expansion to the south. VP-772 started flare-dropping missions on June 12, 1951, according to Allan G. Blue's *The B-24 Liberator*. The flares they dropped illuminated targets for Marine night fighters. VP-9 joined the flare runs, as communist traffic increasingly moved at night. Marine fighter-bombers attacked what the Privateers illuminated. A chute was placed over the rear ventral hatch, from which flares were slipped on orders. More than 150 flares could be carried in the bomb bays of the blue Privateers. The flares were set to ignite at a predetermined altitude, sometimes specifically requested by the attack pilot to match personal preferences. The great range of the Privateer meant one flare-dropper could loiter to service several fighter-bombers in turn, as they expended their ordnance. This sometimes put the Privateers over hostile territory for as much as 4–8hr, said to be the longest duration any American combat planes spent over enemy areas in Korea.

## Reserve Privateers

Naval Reserve squadron VP-981 was taking on Privateers at Naval Air Station (NAS) Seattle by December 1952. Other Reserve squadrons acquiring Privateers in this era are listed in the chart:

| Naval Air Station | Tail Code Letter |
|---|---|
| Seattle, WA | T |
| Glenview, IL | V |
| Memphis, TN | M |
| New York, NY | R |
| Miami, FL | H |
| Olathe, KS | K |

## Last Loss?

A Nationalist Chinese PB4Y-2 allegedly used to resupply guerrillas was shot down by Burmese fighters in 1961, records indicate. This must rank as the last combat loss of an American-made heavy patrol bomber of the World War II era.

## Red Tails in the Sunset

The last Privateers in US Navy service were the rich red QP-4B drones used at the Pacific Missile Test Center (PMTC), Point Mugu, California. On January 18, 1964, the one Privateer remaining in the Navy was downed in a missile test, according to an account in

*Called Liberator C-IX, this RY-3 (JT973) was photographed in an RAF livery on November 4, 1947. The British received 26 of the 33 RY-3s built.*

*British RY-3 numbers were JT973, JT975-998, and JV936. Peter M. Bowers Collection*

*IAF B-24s served as late as 1968, and provided a wealth of nose-turret Libera-* *tors for museums and warbird collections. Indian Air Force*

B-24M 44-51228 in post-1947 star configuration. Used for ice research, 228
went on permanent display at Lackland
AFB, Texas, at the end of its career in
the early 1950s—the last Liberator in
US Air Force service. Later Ford knife-
edge canopy and modified nose contours are visible. Peter M. Bowers Collection

P4Y-1P number 65356 (the B was
deleted from nomenclature when this
photo was taken) served into the 1950s.
Hooded turbo-superchargers are evident. Peter M. Bowers Collection

*Privateers of VP-871 prepared to leave snowy Atsugi, Japan, for nocturnal combat flare missions over Korea that could sometimes last 12hr. The squadron flew almost 1,000 sorties over Korea for an eight-month period in 1951–1952.* James Tiburzi Collection

the *Missile,* the newspaper for PMTC. The story said the Navy was down to two Privateers by mid-December 1963. Known by the call signs Opposite 31 (sometimes nicknamed *Lucky Pierre*) and Opposite 35 (sometimes known as

*US Coast Guard P4Y-2G number 66302 flew postwar search missions with scanners' seats in modified nose, waist, and tail locations. Number 66302 later entered the civilian market as fire bomber number N2871G, operated by Hawkins and Powers Aviation as Tanker 121.* Peter M. Bowers Collection

*This red Privateer target drone, BuNo. 59872, spent its final days at Point Mugu, California.* Jim Morrow Collection

*Clyde*), the red drones occasionally flew manned transport runs out to the PMTC airstrip on San Nicholas Island when the regular C-54 was down for maintenance.

On December 18, 1963, Opposite 31 went airborne on a NOLO (No Live Operator) drone mission from San Nicholas. Point Mugu's test squadron, VX-4, fired missiles at the red Privateer as its remote operator maneuvered between 500 and 1,000ft in altitude to evade the armaments hurled at the QP-4B. San Nicholas was packed with

spectators that day. To their vocal delight, Opposite 31 continued to fly even after receiving a direct hit from a missile that ripped into a starboard bomb bay door. According to the published account, the last fighter attack on the test program that day launched a missile that cut the right wing off the Privateer, which rolled over and splashed down in the Pacific in a shower of sea foam.

## Civilianizing the Warplane

Liberators and Privateers were examined for their civil aviation potential after the war. In addition to the former Navy PB4Y-1 ferried to Oregon, and later sold into South America, several LB-30s, C-87s, and converted B-24s made it into the civilian market. LB-

30s (see chapter 2 for more details on the LB-30) flew passengers and freight for several companies in various parts of the postwar world. Stripped of armament and armor plate, and not required to hold formation at 22,000ft or more, civilianized Liberators worked well.

In the 1950s, a commercial aircraft broker in southern California advertised several LB-30s for sale. At least two B-24s are thought to have flown as cargo haulers in Bolivia up to the 1960s, and a few seldom-photographed Liberators plied the 1950s skies between American airports in an era before warbird spotters tracked all such movements.

Privateers found a home with firefighting companies. The PB4Y-2s could

carry more retardant than could B-17s. From the late 1950s to the present—1993—Privateers have fought fires in the United States. By the 1970s, the survivors of this dangerous peacetime profession had been upgraded to "Super Privateer" status with Wright Double Cyclone engines and nacelles from B-25 Mitchell bombers replacing the Pratt & Whitney R-1830s and their characteristic long, oval cowlings. The R-2600 engine packages add performance at altitude, which can be critical to a Privateer in the mountains on a hot day, when the air thins out, with much the same effect as rarified air at high altitude.

## Civilian Privateer Tail Numbers

Following is a compilation of many of the known civilian Privateers flown in the United States. Details about the aircraft are provided where known:

*N6813D, BuNo. 59876:* Former US Coast Guard plane. Airframe less engines, in peeling white paint, was parked at Grass Valley, California, in the late 1960s, with spray booms attached to wings; the aircraft was later flown out and operated as a fire bomber by Hawkins and Powers Aviation, Greybull, Wyoming, as tanker No. 125 on fire contracts in the western United States, including Alaska. It was

*Hawkins and Powers Aviation's Tanker 124, modified over the years with Coast Guard-style nose, clear-view canopy, and B-25 engines and nacelles, was poised for firefighting duty at Boise, Idaho, in the summer of 1989. Frederick A. Johnsen*

ditched off the north end of Vancouver Island in 1975 while returning from Alaskan fire duty. It was later rebuilt for static display by the Yankee Air Museum, Willow Run, Michigan.

*N6816D:* Operated by Wenairco of Wenatchee, Washington, as a fire bomber in the 1960s and later sold, al-

*Clipped wing tips housed cameras to record performance of missiles launched at this red P4Y-2K drone at Point Mugu, 1962. Final designation of Privateer drones was QP-4B. Sommerich via Peter M. Bowers Collection*

though kept in Wenatchee. Painted white with red trim, and nicknamed *Moby Dick;* later stripped to bare aluminum with orange and white trim. It was assigned tanker No. 42. The aircraft was destroyed on the Wenatchee (Pangborn Field) runway by fire in 1972.

*N6884C (two PB4Y-2s):* First Privateer carrying this civil registration was BuNo. 66284, which crashed in the

summer of 1959. Second Privateer to carry N6884C registration was BuNo. 59701, which was painted aluminum with yellow trim in late 1960s, with tanker No. 84 on tail; acquired by Hawkins and Powers Aviation, Greybull, Wyoming, it was upgraded to Super Privateer engine configuration and had an F-86 canopy placed vertically as its nose cap to improve lower frontal visibility for pilots. Assigned tanker No. 127, this aircraft is still in service as a fire bomber as of 1992.

*N7682C:* Sold surplus with turrets intact; disposition unknown.

*N7962C, BuNo. 59882:* Hawkins and Powers Super Privateer; tanker No. 126. Still active as fire bomber in 1993.

*N2870G, BuNo. 66304:* Hawkins and Powers Super Privateer. Written off in a landing mishap in Ramona, California.

*N2871G, BuNo. 66302:* Hawkins and Powers Super Privateer, Tanker No. 121. Still active as of 1993.

*N2872G, BuNo. 66300:* Hawkins and Powers Super Privateer; tanker No. 124. Still active as of 1993.

*N7620C, BuNo. 66260:* Hawkins and Powers Super Privateer. Still active in 1993.

*N3191G:* A fire bomber seen at Medford, Oregon, in late 1960s, it had early application of flat-sided increased-view canopy. Assigned tanker No. 85, it reportedly crashed in Diamond Lake, Oregon, and was scrapped.

The formative years of American fire bombers found PB4Y-2, registration number N3739G, sharing dusty Arizona ramp space with warbird classics including a TBM, a B-25, and B-17F number N17W in the late 1950s or early 1960s. As of this writing, Privateer N3739G, former BuNo. 59819, is part of the Lone Star Flight Museum in Texas, while B-17F N17W is in the collection of the Museum of Flight, Seattle, Washington. Ken Shake

Air Tanker N6813D got a new lease on life as a static display under restoration by the Yankee Air Museum at the Willow Run, Michigan, airport. Todd Hackbarth Collection

*N3739G, BuNo. 59819:* Converted to fire bomber in early 1960s at Prescott, Arizona, by Flight Enterprises. It was sold to SST Inc. in 1967 and has been operated since 1975 by T and G Aviation, Chandler Field, Arizona. It flew as Tanker No. 30 before being sold in early 1991 to the Lone Star Flight Museum, Galveston, Texas.

## Preserving Liberator Lore

Time has seen increasing efforts to memorialize B-24 and PB4Y aircraft.

There was a time when you could count the preserved Liberators in the United States on the fingers of one hand, and still have three digits unemployed. The Air Force Museum at Wright-Patterson Air Force Base (AFB), Dayton, Ohio, had the foresight to save a combat-veteran B-24D, while Lackland AFB, near San Antonio, Texas, put on display a modified B-24M. Other hulks and pieces remained, but for many years, these two Air Force displays were the only efforts to preserve Liberators. The Pima Air Museum in Tucson, Arizona, doggedly raised money in the 1960s to ferry an IAF B-24J to Tucson as a centerpiece of the then-new museum near Davis-Monthan AFB. Meanwhile, in Texas, fliers who live the good-ol'-boy lifestyle with finesse bought a mongrelized LB-30, initially bedecked it with a Confederate flag, and flew it as part of the tongue-in-cheek Confederate Air Force (CAF), who still operate this oldest surviving Liberator variant as of this writing.

The success of the Pima museum effort at retrieving a former IAF B-24 was repeated for the Canadian National Aeronautical Collection in Ottawa, this time with an L-model. The cost of acquisition and recovery of Liberators would only increase, yet the passion to do so climbed at an even faster rate. Aircraft fancier David Tallichet ob-

*Smoke rushed away from the engines as they were started on David Tallichet's B-24J-95-CF number 44-44272 at Bayview, Washington, in May 1977 during filming of a movie about Navy PB4Y-1 pilot Joe Kennedy. For many years, Tallichet's B-24J was the only flying B-24 in true bomber configuration.* Frederick A. Johnsen

tained in India a twin to the Pima B-24J, which he flew back to the United States. Tallichet also bought two former Canadian B-24Ds that had been dismembered in such a way that their restoration was deemed not feasible. The cockpit section of one of these went to the March Field Museum near Riverside, California, and later to a blossoming air and space museum in Virginia. The characteristic greenhouse from the other was mounted on the nose of the CAF Liberator.

Liberators were in vogue as rare collector items in the 1970s and 1980s. The RAF acquired another former IAF machine, and yet another of the re-markably preserved Indian Liberators was shipped to England by a private buyer who later sold it to Bob Collings in Massachusetts. Under the umbrella of the Air Force Museum Program, Barksdale AFB, Louisiana, secured a slumbering hulk of a Ford-built B-24J in Oklahoma, and sling-loaded it to Louisiana beneath a Skycrane helicopter. Two J-style Liberator nose and cockpit sections were re-imported from Canada by collector and dealer Bruce Orriss. One went to Barksdale as a source of parts, and the other was refurbished in Michigan for display in the state historical society museum in Lansing, where it bears testimony to Ford's role in producing quantities of B-24s in that state during World War II.

A sleeper among the resurrected Liberators was the M-model shipped from Bolivia in 1981 for inclusion in the Castle Air Museum at Castle AFB, Atwater, California. Civilianized many years ago and used as a freight hauler, this Liberator was converted back to bomber status by 1989. Also in the 1980s, Hawkins and Powers Aviation partially restored a languishing PB4Y-2 Privateer, and traded the result to the Navy for inclusion in the naval aviation museum at Pensacola, Florida.

A Privateer fuselage once displayed in the old Ontario Air Museum in southern California was scrapped when the museum was forced to vacate its Ontario airport site, and moved to Chino, California, according to museum director Ed Maloney. A B-24D cockpit and nose formerly employed as a movie prop, with removable fuselage panels, wound up in the storage collection of the National Air and Space Museum at Silver Hill, Maryland. The author purchased the partial cockpit of a PB4Y-2 drone for restoration as a portable museum display, and in Tennessee, the entire fuselage of a Liberator is undergoing refurbishing for static displays around the country.

And the list may not end here—museum groups already are pondering the feasibility of recovering an LB-30 crash-landed by Morrison-Knudsen Construction in Alaska in the 1950s, and a Privateer that slipped beneath the surface of Lake Washington near Seattle in that same decade. Rumors persist of at least one more Liberator to be had from a private owner outside the United States.

From a forlornly discarded and forgotten remnant of the war, the Liberator has recovered lost status to become a key element in several displays and museums in North America and abroad.

Liberators—and significant portions thereof—have been adopted by the following museums and individuals:

## Surviving Liberators

| Variant | Serial | Comments |
|---|---|---|
| Liberator I | AM927 | Flown by CAF, Midlands, Texas |
| B-24 | D-160-CO 42-72843 | On display in Air Force Museum, Dayton, Ohio; nicknamed *Strawberry Bitch* |
| Liberator | HE807(India) | On display in RAF Museum, England |
| B-24 | JKH191 (India) | Owned by Bob Collings, Stowe, Massachusetts |
| B-24 | J-90-CF 44-44175 | On display in Pima Air Museum, Tucson, Arizona |
| B-24 | J-95-CF 44-44272 | Owned by D. Tallichet; put in various museums |
| B-24 | J-25-FO 44-48781 | Eighth AF Museum, Barksdale AFB, Louisiana |
| B-24 | L-20-FO 44-50154 | Canadian National Museum, Ottawa, Ontario |
| B-24 | M-5-CO 44-41916 | Castle Air Museum, Atwater, California |
| B-24 | M-20-FO 44-51228 | Display, Lackland AFB, Texas |
| PB4Y-2 (P4Y-2G) | | For static display by Yankee Air Museum, Willow Run, Michigan; former fire bomber |
| PB4Y-2 | 59819 | Under restoration for flight (R-2600s) by Lone Star Flight Museum, Galveston, Texas |
| PB4Y-2 | | On display at Naval Aviation Museum, Pensacola, Florida; B-25 engine nacelles; modified canopy |
| PB4Y-2 cockpit 59759 | | Under restoration by the author |
| PB4Y-2 forward fuselage | | Under restoration by Ron Sathre, Union City, California |

*Chapter 8*

# Eye of the Beholder

A half-century after its combats, the B-24 needs no excuses, and owes no apologies. Nor do the people associated with these aircraft. The men and women who built and flew Liberators and Privateers remember that time in their lives with a sometimes-frightening clarity and candor; a disarming truthfulness that remains after the years of story-telling embellishments and hindsights are washed away by the tears of remembrance.

What follows is the product of interviews conducted in 1992 with those who knew the Liberator and its kindred aircraft; a human history.

**Ivan Stepnich, Pilot, 66th and 67th BSs, 44th BG**

"I think you had to learn the secret of the B-24," Ivan Stepnich explained. And that secret, celebrated by many Liberator pilots and questioned by others, was "what they called 'being on the step.'" B-24 pilots who believed in the plane's "step" said it was necessary to climb several hundred feet above intended cruising altitude in a loaded B-24, and then drop the nose to pick up speed and establish a proper angle of attack for efficient cruising. Merely

*Carl Stutz was radio operator on* Playmate, *B-24J number 44-40791 in the 494th BG in the Pacific in 1945. Larry Davis Collection*

climbing to altitude and leveling off in a heavy B-24 was said to result in a nose-high mushing flight with attending bad traits ranging from reduced forward visibility to general sluggishness. Engineers and pilots may argue whether the step premise is valid, but one thing is evident: by visualizing the step concept, and flying accordingly, some B-24 pilots were able to trim and operate their Liberators more efficiently.

Ivan Stepnich was moved from B-17 training to B-24s at Gowen Field, Idaho, in the summer of 1943. Finishing up at Pocatello, Idaho, Stepnich and his crew were routed as replacements to Camp Shanks, New York, where they boarded the converted luxury liner *Queen Elizabeth* for the voyage to the United Kingdom in the fall of 1943. Pressed into service as a troop ship, the ocean liner's plumbing had some emergency wartime concessions, and hot showers were taken with salt water. Lieutenant Stepnich shared a stateroom with several other men. He commented, "As an officer it wasn't too bad for me." Days were spent in the large ship's auditorium, where many card tables saw heavy use hour after hour.

Train rides through Scotland and England carried Stepnich and crew from the *Queen Elizabeth* to a transition field at Chedington. He still did not know to which combat group he

and his crew would be assigned. The orders came for the 44th BG at Shipdam. The 44th was the oldest AAF Liberator bomb group, highly experienced, and woven into the fabric of the mighty Eighth AF.

From the start, Stepnich's plane was *P-Bar,* both as a radio call sign and an unofficial nickname, because the individual letter *P,* underlined with a bar, was this B-24's identifier within the 44th BG system of markings. *P-Bar* was either a B-24H or B-24J. Stepnich flew his bomber routinely at 19,000–21,000ft over Europe, with Eighth AF B-17s going higher. The lower Liberators sometimes bore the brunt of antiaircraft hits. "The closer you are to the flak, the more accurate it is," Stepnich explained. And the fighter opposition was "the best there was." The Luftwaffe, taking advantage of early-morning conditions which had the B-24s facing the eastern rising sun, would make head-on attacks out of the sun. "Before our gunners could even pull the triggers, they [the German fighters] were gone. Then we'd see the unlucky ones go down." As sobering as the sight of falling B-24s was, Stepnich and the rest of the 44th BG plowed ahead, gradually getting accustomed to the deadly routine. "We were regularly hit with flak and fighters," he added.

Stepnich took pride in his airmanship, and attentively flew as briefed to achieve a smooth form-up over Eng-

*Liberator crews learned they could slow their tricycle-gear B-24s by unfurling parachutes from the waist windows if they anticipated brake loss. This Douglas-built B-24H flew with the Eighth AF's 466th BG.* Jeff Ethell Collection

land. Following the briefed headings and altitudes through the often-overcast English skies was important. "Everybody had to fly it just right or you could have a mid-air," he said. As the winter of 1943 bore down on the crews, flying in the already-cold upper

atmosphere, Stepnich was pleased to find the electrically heated flying clothing worked as advertised.

During Stepnich's combat flying, the number of missions needed for completion of a tour was raised from 25 to 30. He logged a mission on February 25, 1944, that nearly cut his combat career short. *P-Bar* was part of a formation dispatched across France and into Germany to drop bombs on an aircraft plant at Furth, near Nurnberg. The Initial Point (IP) was made with no undue problems, and the target was bombed from only 18,000ft, with a true

airspeed of 185 knots. Navigator G. R. Henriet's flight plan logged bombs away at 1403. As *P-Bar* and the formation turned left off the target, Henriet wrote: "Good hits all over. . . Lots of fires."

Then came one burst of flak immediately abeam *P-Bar,* puncturing the Liberator from nose to tail and cranking it over sideways as Stepnich wrestled the big bomber back to level. The tail gunner was hit in the shoulder, while up front, Stepnich and his flight engineer each caught flak from the one burst. The oil-fed propeller governor on

No. 3 engine was damaged, and that engine was shut down but windmilling because the governor could no longer feather the blades. This added drag to the stricken Liberator and contributed to a staggering loss of altitude, compounded by a flak-weakened No. 2 engine that gave about half power. Punctured hydraulics, strange noises, and faltering powerplants held Stepnich's attention as he initially tried to maintain his briefed exit route back to England. *P-Bar* lost 10,000ft before stabilizing only 8,000ft over a very hostile Germany. At a point southeast of Wurzburg, Stepnich turned south, because neutral Switzerland was closer than trying to run clear across the rest of Germany and enemy-occupied France at 8,000ft, alone. Southwest of Heilbron, 37min after bombs-away, Stepnich knew he could never get the injured *P-Bar* high enough to cross the mountains into Switzerland. He took up a new heading westward, laboring across Germany and France.

During *P-Bar*'s ordeal, one German fighter pressed an attack, but broke it off. Other enemy fighters were seen in the air, but did not engage the lone aircraft. Stepnich set up westward headings based on his navigator's advice. The route was south of that flown by the rest of the group, and that may have helped spare *P-Bar* from attacks aimed at the large group of B-24s. The crew began jettisoning guns and ammunition over the English Channel to further lighten *P-Bar;* they had to keep the weapons while over enemy territory in case they were spotted. A fighter field on English soil, too short for a Liberator and with uphill terrain at the far end of the runway, was Stepnich's only alternative to ditching.

Nursing a damaged B-24 back to England on little more than two engines, with gas running low, it was natural for Ivan Stepnich to hoard altitude. On final approach to the short fighter strip, he realized the bomber was still too high, and would consume too much of the precious runway if he tried to land from this height. Stepnich initiated a go-around, over the protests of his copilot and flight engineer, both of whom feared *P-Bar* was about to run out of gas. Stepnich prevailed, preferring to take his chances on the fuel remaining rather than pile up into the

hill at the end of the runway. His gamble paid off. Unknown to the crew at the time, one of the B-24's main tires was destroyed by the flak burst, and this may have saved the plane and crew as they jammed the damaged Liberator into the cramped fighter strip. The useless wheel dragged the B-24 to a stop before running into the hill. Afterward, the flight engineer measured only about 40 gallons remaining in the limping Liberator's tanks. Old *P-Bar* was repaired, but Stepnich doubted it ever saw combat again. But Ivan Stepnich and crew went to war soon—in a replacement *P-Bar*.

Ivan Stepnich flew with finesse, and fully embraced the B-24 Liberator. Unlike some Liberator pilots, Stepnich enjoyed formation flying most of all: "That was a thing of beauty," he said. The customary stiffness of the B-24's controls may have aided his formation technique because the stiffness prevented overcontrolling. "You had to exert plenty of positive force and therefore you didn't overcorrect," explained Stepnich.

His 30 missions finished, Stepnich went to Eighth AF headquarters as an engineering officer, where he worked on a war-weary B-24H nicknamed *Hap Hazard.* This B-24 was the test bed for a revised nose with a boosted twin .50cal gun mount made by Bell in a

*Same art as on* Playmate, *but a different artist rendered this version of a Varga girl as* Shoo Shoo Baby, *B-24H number 42-95197 of the 446th BG, Eighth AF. Nicknames and pieces of pin-up art were repeated on B-24s and other warplanes throughout the USAAF. Doug Remington Collection*

modified B-24D greenhouse. Stepnich, by then a captain, was on the crew that flew the test bed back to the United States for inspection by AAF and factory officials at sites like Wright Field.

## Mercer R. "Ray" Markman, Pilot, 759th BS, 459th BG

"All I remember is a great big cross going by my side . . . the biggest black cross I'd ever seen!" Lt. Ray Markman saw the flash of German insignia as a Bf 109 roared past his Liberator's cockpit after making a head-on pass that left Markman's ball turret gunner dead in his turret, and the B-24's No. 2 Pratt & Whitney engine shot out. It was Markman's first mission as a new pilot in the Fifteenth AF, April 23, 1944. "That's when you realize they're playing for keeps," he commented. The target was a Messerschmitt plant at Bad Voslau, Austria.

With one engine out and a full load of bombs, Markman's B-24 lost alti-

*Ray Markman, left, inspected a German 20mm slug that lodged in his B-24.* Ray Markman Collection

tude, its bomb bay doors already open in anticipation of impending bomb release. All eyes were on the lead bombardier; when he dropped, the rest of the formation would drop. Markman faced a new peril as he struggled to keep up with the formation: If he slipped back as he lost altitude, the bombs of a Liberator still at formation altitude could smash into his crippled B-24. Gamely, Markman tried to keep his B-24 directly under the hole in the sky where he had been before the fighter attack. He flew between 100 and 200ft beneath the rest of the formation. Bombs fell all around his Liberator, and his bombardier toggled his bombs in time.

With an incapacitated ball turret jammed in the extended position and one engine shut down, Markman could not hope to stay with the lightened formation as they turned away from the target area. He and his crew were alone, over enemy-annexed Austria, heading for the Adriatic Sea as quickly as their slowed bomber would allow. Occasionally, lone P-38 Lightning fighters, dispatched on other sorties, would form up with Markman and offer a few minutes' protection before accelerating on to their assigned duties.

Markman landed the crippled B-24 back at his airstrip in Italy with the damaged ball turret extended, its gunner still entombed inside. He instructed other available crew members to be as far forward in the plane as possible once a safe touchdown was achieved, to keep the low-slung B-24 from rocking back and dragging the ball turret on the runway. Markman, his bombardier, and navigator were aboard this Liberator with other experienced men from different crews. For him and his crew members, it was a stark baptism of fire.

When Ray Markman was assigned to the Fifteenth AF, he needed to accomplish 50 mission credits to complete a tour of duty. Most missions earned one credit; lengthy, difficult, and dangerous missions could earn two credits. It took him 37 passes over targets to amass 50 mission credits and complete his tour.

Markman's first mission was a taste of things to come. Later, on June 9, 1944, as part of a formation bombing an airfield at Munich, Germany, his camouflaged B-24 was singled out by a lone Bf 109 for a persistent stern attack. With hundreds of Liberators to choose from, it seemed to Markman the German fighter pilot could only see his B-24 that day. The Messerschmitt's 20mm shells frequently flew over and past the B-24, seemingly whizzing through the Liberator's propeller arcs sometimes. One slug lodged in the nose but did not explode; others punched holes in the bomb bay area until the fighter drew close enough for the tail gunner to swap bullets with the German, sending the fighter peeling away streaming light smoke—not enough to confirm a kill.

On the return from Munich, Markman's crew tied parachutes to the waist-gun mounts to slow the damaged B-24 on landing, since its hydraulics—and brakes—were damaged in combat.

The persistent Fifteenth AF attacks on Ploesti's oil refineries included a high-altitude effort on July 15, 1944, that put Markman's Liberator as tail-end Charlie behind the rest of the 459th BG. Pilots dreaded this slot for two reasons: The last bombers were open to stern attacks, and it required far more maneuvering and gasoline to stay in place in the group. The last plane in formation was like the tip of a cracking whip, needing exaggerated movement and acceleration to hold its position, as the planes ahead amplified any perturbations felt by the lead bombers.

Leaving the target area, Markman's formation was momentarily dispersed by a surprise flak barrage. The formation leader had been setting a cruise speed about 5mph faster than normal already, and when Markman advanced his throttles further to regain his place in the formation, all four R-1830 engines began to vibrate and complain. Once again, Ray Markman had no choice but to watch the rest of the formation accelerate and run off ahead as his weakened Liberator lagged back.

Once clear of Yugoslavia, the crew began jettisoning guns and ammunition over the Adriatic. Fuel consumption was a concern as the B-24 descended. Ten miles out from his home field, he received radio landing instructions. Still the Adriatic Sea loomed large ahead and beneath the Liberator. Down to about 2,000ft, the bombardier went aft to jettison the waist windows in preparation for ditching. The left waist hatch got away from him in the slipstream and embedded itself in the horizontal stabilizer, acting as a speed brake for the lame bomber.

All four engines were cutting in and out, delivering fitful power. Markman figured he was only two or three miles from shore, and maybe six miles from the runway, when he knew he had no choice but to ditch. Fishing boats loomed in the windscreen as he maneuvered to avoid them. He cut all four throttles to avoid a surprise burst of power at the last minute from the erratic engines that could yaw the plane dangerously. He leveled out and then dragged in tail-low. Water probably hammered up through the opening where the retracted ball turret nested, ripping the turret free of its mounts and punching it through the right side of the fuselage. The top gunner, seated for ditching in the aft fuselage, may have been carried out with the careening ball turret; he was never found. There was no skipping or planing atop the water; the Liberator slammed to a halt, nose low, but floating. The tail section was broken and hanging down at an angle from the waist.

Stunned, Markman started to make his way from the cockpit. Somehow, he figured he scrambled through the windscreen, but the sequence of events was blurred. He found himself underwater, and pondering drowning, until he opened his eyes in the salt water and saw he was near the Number Two engine. Markman hoisted himself up on the prop dome of that engine and surveyed the wreck topside. An Italian fishing boat neared the floating Liberator, and he slipped back in the water to make sure all the crew was out of the B-24. He found his bombardier, dazed by the crash, still seated in the tail section where he had assumed his ditching position. Markman repeatedly called to the bombardier to leave the fuselage via the gaping hole torn by the ball turret in the right side of the fuselage. The drama of the precariously floating Liberator heightened the tension as the still-groggy bombardier finally heeded his call and abandoned the plane for the Italian boat. Everybody but the unfortunate top-turret gunner had survived.

Aboard the boat, the crew members removed soaked flight jackets and boots, which Markman noticed the boat

*Ray Markman's first combat mission, in Leila Nell, resulted in this muscle-powered engine change.* Ray Markman Collection

crew quietly putting away, never to be seen again by the bedraggled fliers. The men transferred to a British torpedo boat, which took them to shore.

Not until a 1992 reunion with his flight engineer did Ray Markman learn why some events of the ditching were unclear in his memory: The engineer, seeing his preoccupied pilot emerge from the sea with a bleeding gash on his forehead, administered a morphine shot that Markman was unaware he had received until 48 years later!

Over a month later, after a stay in the hospital, and time off for rest and recuperation, plus a trip north to the fighting front as a sightseer aboard a B-25, Ray Markman again hoisted a B-24 into the air on a mission August 20. He hadn't lost any of his finesse with a B-24 in the time he was away, but he remembered, "I was a little nervous about flying over water. It took a few missions for me to get over that."

The airfield where Ray Markman lived and flew was in an Italian wheat field. The British provided antiaircraft guns for protection, although an inbound Do 217 bomber manned by Yugoslavian defectors was never shot at; it crash-landed nearby after circling until it ran out of gas. The nearest town was Cerignola, in the Foggia area. The officers of his crew shared a tent, and his enlisted aircrew shared

another, remodeled with wooden walls made from crates. Every morning at about 3:30 a jeep driver, honking the vehicle's horn, ambled through the living area waking those crew members who had a mission—and distracting everyone else.

Ray Markman was unusual among B-24 pilots—before joining the AAF in 1942, he worked for Consolidated Aircraft in San Diego, building Liberators.

Markman said the thing he liked least about the B-24 was "the flight deck was awfully crowded."

What Ray Markman liked most was the dependable Pratt & Whitney engines, and the unusually comfortable design of the rudder pedals, with cradles for the heels of the feet. He also liked the tricycle gear, which he said made the B-24 easier to land than tailwheel aircraft.

### Louis Mladenovic, Chetnik, Yugoslavia

"We couldn't talk; I imagine they were pretty well shook up," Louis Mladenovic recalled. Mladenovic had just helped rescue and hide members of a B-24 crew from the German patrol that was looking for them. Gradually communications improved, and the fierce Chetniks proved to be loyal friends, willing to take great risks to guide the Liberator aircrew back to safety.

The Chetniks were legendary in Yugoslavia as mountain people who defied the Turks centuries before Nazi Germany invaded Yugoslavia. In 1941, Louis Mladenovic shed his Yugoslavian Army uniform and blended back into the fabric of his hometown of Kragujevac after the German takeover. That July, the Nazi regime executed 3,000–4,000 Yugoslavians in the nearby town of Krajlevo, including Mladenovic's sister and the third-grade class she taught. The first week of October, the Germans rounded up thousands of people in his home town and began randomly counting off their hostages in groups of 100 people. One group was set free; the next executed; and on through the captives in a fiendish math exercise intended to terrorize the citizenry. Mladenovic had missed the round-up; now his father urged him to leave Kragujevac, to escape the fate of his sister, or of his younger brother, a watchmaker's apprentice, who was shipped to Germany as forced labor in an aircraft instrument factory.

Louis Mladenovic went to live with an uncle for about six or eight months, where he learned about the Chetniks' armed resistance to the German occupation. After local Chetnik leaders were convinced he would not betray their cause, Mladenovic joined forces with them near Boljevac in the late summer of 1942. When asked why he chose to fight the Germans, his answer was succinct: "Why did they kill my young sister for no reason?" Instructed in the ways of train bombing by British commandos who parachuted in to teach the hardy Chetniks, Mladenovic was part of a unit of 80 resistance fighters in his region. About 200 local citizens additionally took up arms at night to bolster the Chetnik forces.

Sometimes Mladenovic hiked past the locust trees, and higher beyond the oaks and maples, into open sheep meadows and up to the rocky top of a 10,000ft mountain where he could watch the incredible Fifteenth AF armada winging toward Ploesti repeatedly in the spring of 1944. One such sunny mountain day, he sat back and tallied 350 American heavy bombers before he stopped counting them all. At this height, the constant roar of the bombers shook the earth, and caused rocks to loosen and roll downhill.

When not awe-struck by the armada, Mladenovic and his colleagues fought an ongoing war of attack and sabotage against the occupying Germans throughout this period.

Into this melting pot of Yugoslavian patriots parachuted B-24 pilot Thomas K. Oliver and eight members of his crew on May 6, 1944. Oliver, who paid homage to his own superstition by always carrying a slip of paper with his estimated time of arrival back at base, was surprised when that talisman whipped out through the cockpit window as he taxied out for takeoff that day. Later, Oliver recalled, "I remember the flight engineer saying, 'We didn't need that, did we?' I bravely said 'No' and on we went." The B-24 that day was not Oliver's usual mount, which had been nicknamed *The Fighting Mudcat*. The replacement ship would not outlast the day. After successfully bombing the Campina marshaling yards near the Ploesti oil fields, Oliver and his 459th BG compatriots took flak and fighter damage as the lead group for the Fifteenth AF that day. "Shortly after 'bombs away' No. 3 engine was losing oil pressure," Oliver recounted. "I tried to feather it, without success. . . . The prop governor had been hit and was hanging by one bolt. The drag and vibration forced us to slow down and lag behind the formation."

Now No. 3 engine seized after losing all oil. "The vibration was horrendous," Oliver explained. "The right wing shook in a sine wave pattern as though one took one end of a rope and tied it to a tree, and then gave a good shake to the other end." Suddenly the propeller began free-wheeling, probably with the failure of the overwrought reduction gear. "Things went more smoothly for a while," Oliver said. But then No. 4 engine began registering a drop in oil pressure. With no desire to repeat the problems of the runaway engine, Oliver feathered No. 4 while he still had engine oil pressure available to drive the feathering mechanism.

"With two engines dead on the same side we threw out guns, flak suits . . . anything to reduce weight," he remembered. Holding 8,000ft of altitude, Oliver figured he could limp home, as his navigator charted a course away from known flak batteries.

The crippled Liberator, much lower than normal and chugging over unfamiliar parts of Yugoslavia, chanced upon the town of Bor where a copper and gold mine had its output guarded by a German antiaircraft battery not charted on the navigator's maps. One shell set fire to the B-24's No. 2 engine, and perforated the bomb bay doors like the holes in a salt shaker. The only choice was parachuting from the plane. "As I tumbled through the air I remember saying to myself that even if the parachute didn't open, I was no worse off than when I was in the plane."

Oliver landed in the midst of a Serbian picnic celebrating the annual summertime return of the Chetniks to the mountains—a legendary event dating back to the time of the Turks. The B-24 crashed with a brilliant explosion on a hill near Bogovina, about 20 or 25mi distant from the mine at Bor.

As German armored vehicles raced toward the scene of the crash, Louis Mladenovic and his fellow Chetniks, aided by local farmers, safely hid nine of Oliver's crew. Crashing shortly after noon, the Liberator aircrew were dangerously close to being apprehended by the Germans by about 4pm. "I picked up two" of the crew members, he recalled. "We had them all together after two or three days."

The next day, May 7, 1944, another stricken B-24 swooped over the leafy trees and open fields of northeastern Yugoslavia, looking for a place to forceland. "The second plane, we saw him coming down. . . . As the crow flies it wasn't three kilometers from the other one," Mladenovic said. The pilot managed to put the Liberator down safely enough to spare his entire crew of 10. The left wing was destroyed in the crash-landing. (Records indicate the 454th BG lost two B-24s on that date; this may be the origin of the second B-24 downed in Mladenovic's area.)

After both crews were sheltered by the Chetniks, a knowledgeable member of the second crew—almost certainly a gunner—volunteered to take the Chetniks back to the wreck to strip out the waist guns and ammunition for continued use against the Germans on the ground. Wrecks were dangerous for Yugoslavians to visit because of German prohibitions. At night, aided by flashlights, the American and about 10 Chetniks returned to the crash and carted off the two .50cal waist guns, in their E-12 recoil adaptors and yokes. Six full ammunition boxes were packed away from the wreck as well. Back in the relative safety of the Chetnik hideout, the American taught his protectors how to clean and service the big Browning machine guns. A local blacksmith welded tube tripods to mount the guns, which were then packed into battle on the X-frame saddles of horses. The guns rode on the horses' backs in the crook of the X-frame, with ammunition boxes tied to the sides of the saddle frame. Ring-and-bead gunsights intended for framing Messerschmitts in flight were now used against German mortar and machine gun positions.

Eventually, the B-24 aircrews were smuggled out of Yugoslavia. Some crossed the Adriatic in fishing boats bound for Italy; others scrambled aboard C-47s that landed on an improvised sod airstrip tamped out by the Chetniks on a hilltop. Oliver returned to his base in Italy 96 days after parachuting from his B-24. As he entered the C-47, Oliver and many other crew members being evacuated tossed their shoes back, as a token of appreciation, for use by the strapped Chetniks in their continuing guerrilla war against the Germans.

Louis Mladenovic was commander of a machine-gun group that used one of the B-24 weapons for three or four pitched fights with the Germans before expending all the ammunition. He said the authoritative report of the big .50cal got the Germans' attention. "We used [the B-24 guns] mostly against the other machine guns and mortars. . . . We cut the trees with them," Mladenovic said.

Even though the aircrews had long been passed from friend to friend in Yugoslavia, the Germans evidently had bad information that Mladenovic's Chetnik outfit still harbored the Americans in August 1944. On August 16 the Germans engaged the Chetniks, possibly in search of the Americans,

and possibly because (as he remembered it) some Chetniks had shot a Luftwaffe fighter pilot as he wafted to earth in his parachute. Armored German vehicles supported the attack on the Chetniks, which began about 7pm and lingered until about 4am the next morning. As gun crew captain, Mladenovic warned his gunner manning the .50cal to keep his head down. When next he looked over at the gunner, he saw the top of his head blown away by a German bullet. Mladenovic took up firing with the B-24 gun until the last round was shot.

Out of ammunition, Mladenovic ran from the now-useless weapon. He thought he felt a tug at his British-style uniform jacket, but there was no pain to tell him a German bullet had hit him in the back, passing between his ribs and exiting his chest. He continued running about 200ft before he noticed blood and foam spouting from his chest. At that point, he collapsed—far enough from the battle to be left for dead by the Germans. A Chetnik subsequently propped Mladenovic on a horse and assumed he was dead, taking him to a farmhouse for burial. In the cellar of the rural home, Mladenovic stirred, to the surprise of the occupants. Local women soaked cloths in homemade brandy and bound his chest. It was the only medication he received for his wound. Seven days after being shot, Louis Mladenovic, walking with a stick for a crutch, carried a British grease-gun automatic weapon as he was once again on the run with the Chetniks.

Nearly 50 years after he helped save American Liberator crews from capture, Louis Mladenovic, living in the United States, succeeded in contacting Thomas Oliver, the pilot of the first B-24 involved. In a very tangible way, the B-24 touched the life of Louis Mladenovic in Yugoslavia.

## Ted Small, Pilot, 397th BS, 6th BG

"My opinion of what made the B-24 reliable was the Pratt & Whitney engines," commented Ted Small. Small's tour in Liberators began right out of multi-engine school, and before he had time for any formal B-24 phase training. He was already in Tucson to begin Liberator pilot training when he was

picked to be a copilot in the Canal Zone's 6th BG. In May of 1943, Small joined up with the 397th BS, learning the ropes from the right seat of the unit's weary old LB-30s.

Small found the LB-30 to be a mixed blessing. Lighter than subsequent B-24s, the LB-30 enjoyed a performance edge in some phases of flight. But wear-and-tear had taken their toll on the LBs. Unlike later B-24s, the LB-30s were not fitted with a gasoline "putt-putt" power unit. Instead, the LB-30s relied on the strength of two batteries for start-up electrical power. The added power drain imposed by the use of Curtiss Electric propellers was a source of problems. "We had a terrible time with the Curtiss Electric propellers on the LB-30s," Small recalled. When the batteries gave out at the end of the runway, the loss of electrical power allowed the brakes on the electric propeller assemblies to relax, causing the prop blades to go out of pitch.

Small was philosophical about flying well-worn LB-30s: "We felt bad to have such poor airplanes, but we felt the guys in actual combat needed the good ones more than we did." Parts were scarce, and a local depot in the Canal Zone was not high on Small's list for turning out reliable overhauled parts—including the vaunted Pratt & Whitneys, which sometimes had to be replaced multiple times before a good overhauled powerplant could be found. Gasoline leaks in the wing tanks eventually grounded all the squadron's LB-30s until the depot could fix them.

Ted Small spoke with genuine emotion as he recalled bailing out of a burning LB-30 on July 15, 1943, over Panama. It was a flier's nightmare; after aborting a radar search mission because No. 1 engine was not producing power, and being chewed out for returning to base when the problem could not be duplicated on a ground check of the LB-30, copilot Small and five other members of the crew reboarded the old bomber for a test hop, in anticipation of returning to base for the rest of the crew if the hop proved the plane was okay. The test showed the balky engine still was not developing proper power, and as the pilot headed the LB-30 on downwind leg of the landing pattern, the engine began to burn.

*Ted Small smiled for the camera as he posed with a 6th BG LB-30,* The Groundhog. *Note the sea-search mottling on sides and undersurfaces that may consist of white sprayed irregularly over neutral gray, although the background color under the white has not been positively identified. Upper surfaces on LB-30s in Panama typically were mixed patterns, probably consisting of olive drab or medium green and dark earth.* Ted Small Collection

Fire extinguishers only caused the blaze to falter momentarily before blistering back to life. The electric prop would not feather. The pilot climbed as the problem unfolded, affording the aircrew an altitude of about 900ft from which to bail out.

Seemingly unrelated chance events strung together to save Ted Small's life that hot July day over Rio Hato's airfield. Earlier, his parachute got soaked with water, rendering it unusable. Ex-tra parachutes were in the waist of the Liberator, left by the other crew members still waiting on the ground. Small recalled how his pilot told him to go back and jump with one of the spare chutes, which is exactly what the young lieutenant, along with three other crew members, were able to do. One of the men who jumped died because his parachute burned. The survivors all left from the waist of the LB-30. Up front, for reasons Ted Small can never know, his pilot did not leave the cockpit even after telling him to do so. When the burning Liberator crashed, the pilot and radio operator were still in their seats. Small still wondered as of this writing if the pilot thought he could save the burning bomber and land it. But the circumstances were aerodynamically unhealthy—the dead engine was on the left wing, and the traffic pattern was a left turn onto final approach, which could have proven disastrous to a Liberator with shy power on the wing inside the turn.

Small and the other survivors were grounded a couple days while an officer conducted a brusque investigation of the mishap, and the men held funerals for their fellow crew members.

Soon Ted Small was flying again, first as a copilot whenever the brass needed him to fill that seat on VIP flights, and then as the first pilot for his old crew mates.

The 6th BG (and VI Bomber Command after November 1, 1943) had the charter of providing long-range bombing power in the event an enemy fleet dared approach the Panama Canal. Almost as a secondary role, the Liberators of the 6th assisted the US Navy in patroling both the Pacific Ocean and the Caribbean—the former for signs of a Japanese fleet and the latter for the very real threat of German submarines.

The old LB-30s had a Bendix radar that Small disdained for being hard on the eyes of the operator. Later B-24s in Panama had newer radars. During spikes in U-boat activity in the Caribbean, these AAF Liberators helped the Navy patrol the area. It was on one such mission that Ted Small had his only probable enemy contact. "I had one disappearing radar contact," he recalled, saying the radar echo—or the submarine it probably represented—was not visible by the time the Liberator made its run over the water at 500ft. The next day, a Colombian destroyer sank a submarine in that area, Small was told.

When patrolling Pacific approaches to the Panama Canal, Small and the rest of the 6th crews on those missions would fly from Baltra in the Galapagos Islands, and then to San Jose, Guatemala, where they remained overnight. The next day, they would fly the leg back to the Galapagos. Sometimes, two Liberators launched, doubling the swath of observation. Another track took the 6th BG from Galapagos to overfly a part of Peru about 400mi distant, then swinging back north and recovering at Baltra.

In 1944, B-24Ds began supplanting the tired LB-30s. These were followed by J-models and some Ford-built B-24Ms that the crews called "Tin Lizzies" in reference to their auto-maker ancestry.

Ted Small, originally an enlisted AAF radio operator after joining up on December 17, 1941, passed exams to enable him to become a flying cadet, and thence a commissioned officer and pilot. Not long after the war, while on a 30-day leave back in the States, Small was offered separation from the service rather than his projected return to Panama. He settled back into the peaceful, if vigorous, agrarian lifestyle near Walla Walla, Washington.

But Ted Small never shed his interest in the Liberators that he knew so intimately for more than two years in the cockpit, down in Central America's largely overlooked war zone.

## Carl A. Stutz, Radio Operator, 867th BS, 494th BG, Seventh AF

"I didn't know how to boogie-woogie or anything, but I knew radio," recalled Carl Stutz. Sergeant Stutz built a crystal radio when he was 12 years old, and excelled in math and science in high school. That, he believed, helped propel him into the AAF instead of the regular Army when he was drafted out of high school in 1943.

As an enlisted radio operator, Stutz saw double duty, as right waist gunner on the B-24J nicknamed *Playmate*. The 494th BG was the last Liberator bomb group formed, rumbling into combat in November 1944. By early 1945, after

receiving B-24 crew training at Muroc, California, and crewing a brand-new B-24M from Hamilton Field, near San Francisco, to Hawaii, Stutz and his crew found themselves flying combat in an older, yet reliable, B-24J when their brand-new bomber was taken in Hawaii. Stutz said his crew was flown to Palau in ATC C-54s and C-46s in stages, to begin racking up a string of 26 combat missions before the Japanese surrender in mid-August 1945 cut short this crew's career as Liberator warriors.

Stutz' crew was given B-24J number 44-40791, with a fetching Varga girl lounging on the left side of the nose. His crew added the name *Playmate*. Unlike some crews, Stutz flew all his combat in that one B-24, piloted by Lt. James Fair.

The 494th bombed targets in the Philippines from the Palau Islands before taking up residence at Yontan, on newly occupied Okinawa.

On a typical mission, would pretune the B-24's tube-radio receivers and transmitters for optimum signal. He knew this to be an art. "If you pulled too much [power on the liaison radio transmitter] the plate on the tube would get red. . . . If you mis-tune a transmitter, it just melts down inside," he explained. Once tuned, the command radio receivers could be operated by the pilot, who had "coffee-grinder" control cranks for tuning frequencies as needed. Stutz' office was in the forward fuselage, just behind the copilot's seat. The command radio and radio compass gear were located aft of the wing.

For the first part of a mission, Stutz stayed at his radio post. On flights in a noncombat area, like the ferry flight to Hawaii, he made position calls hourly, based on coordinates furnished by the navigator. This helped plot the location of the B-24 in the event of its disappearance. In combat, he maintained radio silence except for those missions in which his was the lead crew. Then it was his responsibility to send off a coded strike assessment, using the Morse key, as soon as the target was hit. The bombardier would provide the assessment data, including an estimate of the percentage of bombs on target.

Typically, each mission had a zone in which fighter opposition could occur. As *Playmate* entered this zone, it was Stutz' responsibility to leave his radio post and occupy the drafty right waist-gun position. But his combats in 1945 did not yield any duels with enemy fighters. Sometimes, the lack of expected enemy aerial opposition prompted the Liberators to fly unescorted. Mustang fighters were available if hostile air action was anticipated. "We had about 30 P-51s with us on some missions," Stutz recalled. "They would not let a B-24 shoot down a fighter if they were around. They wanted to get credit for it, and we sure appreciated it. . . . A fighter never did get in to us."

Sergeant Stutz did face flak, especially over parts of the Philippines like Zamboanga. "When you can hear them, they're close," he added.

Records from Stutz' missions show that *Playmate* typically bombed from altitudes ranging between 9,000 to 12,000ft—suicidal over Europe, but feasible against some Japanese-held targets. These low altitudes precluded the need for anyone to be on oxygen.

Overall, Stutz said his combat tour "was the smoothest 26 missions."

## David Gale Behunin, Tail Gunner, VPB-106

"The first time I opened up, I couldn't believe the damage I was doing to that ship," recalled Dave Behunin. Behunin was comfortable and competent in the Consolidated (MPC) tail turret of his lanky PB4Y-2 Privateer. As part of Navy squadron VPB-106, he saw the war backward, as it reeled beneath his '4Y-2 and disappeared, sometimes in a hail of tracer fire.

"Our primary goal was weather reporting and keeping track of major [Japanese] ship movements," Behunin explained. They were barred from attacking major warships because of the vessels' competent defenders and massive firepower, but, said Behunin, "If we wanted to we could take out the picket boats." The pickets radioed American movements back to Japan, and sinking them deprived the Japanese of some of their early-warning capability.

Behunin's crew, usually flying their beloved *Tortilla Flat*, as their Pri-

*David Gale Behunin saw the war from the tail turret of the Privateer called* Tortilla Flat. *David Behunin Collection*

vateer was nicknamed, readily engaged picket boats in mast-top attacks. Through 46 combat missions, mostly in this shark-mouthed aircraft, Behunin said he found the picket boats well-armed and well-manned, but poorly trained. The fiercely grinning Privateer only took one hit from a picket boat, when a cannon shell—possibly 20mm—punched through one of the solid-aluminum Hamilton Standard propeller blades.

Behunin recalled anxious moments on his first picket-boat attack. Scanning the sky behind the Privateer from a leisurely 3,000ft over the blue waves, Behunin became aware of the impending fight as the bomber's nose dipped and power was applied for more speed. The dive could be unnerving to a green gunner, not able to see what the pilots could up front. He looked up through the clear canopy of his power turret—up past the tall tail of his Privateer—and was astonished to see all calibers of bullets, running out of energy high in their trajectories, spinning lazily

and tumbling as they flew over the plane. Intercom silence did not reassure Behunin at this point. How could all these rounds miss the big bomber? Were the pilot and copilot already dead, and was he riding a doomed Privateer? "I thought the damn plane was going to fly into the water," he recalled. Just then, Behunin caught sight of .50cal ammunition links whipping beneath the Privateer, as he felt the chattering shudder from the plane's forward guns, and he knew someone was still fighting up front at least.

A new and deadly sound reached Behunin's ears: He could discern the reports from guns on the picket ship as they fired desperately at the Privateer. He figured a ship's bridge was its command center; knock out the bridge, and the ship could only function haphazardly at best. As soon as the Japanese picket boat slipped into the view from his gently curved armor glass, he laced tracers into the bridge. He remembered his surprise at watching the bridge disintegrate in an eroding barrage of .50cal rounds, wood and glass splintering and flying through the air. He kept firing until his tracers dropped short into the sea, signaling the end of his guns' range.

Pontianak, Borneo, was home to a Japanese shipyard for picket boats. Made largely of wood, the ship facility was ripe for incendiaries when Behunin rode in to attack the place in May 1945. Flying upriver to reach Pontianak, the pilot kept the Privateer down near the water. "We flew low enough up the Pontianak River that we could look under the jungle canopy," Behunin explained. There, hidden from view, were Japanese ships which the Privateer gunners strafed even as they roared upriver to their primary target. The treetop Privateer war over Borneo was not without peril. In some locations, the Japanese anticipated Privateer run-ins by placing high-explosive charges in the treetops, to be detonated in the path of an onrushing bomber.

Aviators often acknowledged superstition, especially as a combat tour drew to a close. Eager to survive and rotate home, the crew would cling to favorite sunglasses, or other talismans, as good-luck charms, vital to their continued success in avoiding death in combat. Behunin's replacement crew was already on base at Palawan in the Philippines, and he and the others were anxiously awaiting their release to go home. "By this time, we were all getting pretty superstitious," he explained. A combat mission to Borneo came up. The replacement crew, instead of taking the combat run, opted for a familiarization flight of the area, leaving one more flight over hell to Behunin's crew. It was too ominous; thoughts of dying in Borneo rolled over the crew like storm-driven squalls.

The reality was upbeat as Behunin and crew survived what turned out to be their last combat mission, landing at Palawan and wandering in to hear a radio report of the Japanese surrender. It was August 15. The war was over. Everyone had .38cal revolvers; some had Thompson submachine guns. Down to the beach went celebratory aviators of VPB-106, firing any weapon at hand. "We'd shoot, and shoot, and shoot on the beach," he remembered, marveling that nobody was killed by a stray bullet of celebration.

Behunin liked the Privateer the first time he saw one at Camp Kearney, near San Diego. After one stateside ditching in a storm, and 46 combat missions in the reliable "two-by-four," he felt his initial faith in the plane was well warranted.

## Bill Willard, Bombardier, VPB-102

"I remember when we'd fly out of Iwo we'd pass a squadron of Bettys heading toward Iwo and we'd waggle our wings at each other and keep on going," Bill Willard recalled. Willard joined up with VPB-102 in early 1945. Trained on PB4Y-2 Privateers, which he helped ferry to Tinian, he was disappointed when his crew was given a used Liberator in VPB-102 instead. "We were upset," he recalled, saying the Liberators were beat-up, compared to the tight new Privateers they had just ferried to the combat theater.

Although he was classically trained on the Norden bombsight, the Nordens were taken away about the time he got into combat because the work was low altitude. His new sighting apparatus was an effective but inglorious set of crosshairs on the bombsight window, christened the Rat Trap. Willard perfected his Rat Trap bombing by dropping leftover ordnance for practice during the return legs of patrol sorties. His use of a whale for a target met with swift official disapproval, so other objects were sighted through his aiming window.

Willard's PB4Y-1 typically staged out of Iwo Jima for about two weeks at a time, flying prearranged sector patrols lasting 12–16hr each. Some of the sectors were hot with enemy action; others were safely, boringly, thankfully cold. It was while launching out of Iwo to begin sectors that Willard and crew would sometimes see inbound Japanese bombers. The Liberator crew wanted to light in after the Japanese bombers, but was denied permission to do so. "We'd call back [to base to radio the presence of the Japanese formation], and they'd be waiting for them with P-51s."

The taking of Iwo Jima bypassed fortified Chichi Jima and Haha Jima. One of the tasks of Willard and his PB4Y-1 crew was to patrol the skies aproaching these two Japanese garrisons, to make sure no supply ships got in. "We were always looking for ships." And, in a war without benefit of satellite coverage, the Navy Liberators and Privateers provided updated weather information about conditions encountered on patrol.

Initially, Willard's Liberator carried a lower ball turret. This was swapped for a radome later. After the sensitive Norden bombsight was taken away, the crew installed a fixed 20mm cannon in the nose. Willard avoided being down there when it was in use. His tours into the hot sectors raised fighters, which only sometimes proved willing to engage the blue bomber. Three Japanese planes—Willard thinks they were a Jake and two Zeros—fell before the gunners on his Liberator.

Sometimes tasked to fly air-sea rescue missions, Willard and crew would orbit over ditched crew members—sometimes from B-29s returning from bombing Japan—until friendly submarines could effect the snatch. The effects of seapower impressed him on one air-sea sortie that took his Liberator close to Japan in the waning days of the war. "We were in Tokyo Bay and saw a P-51 go down. They [the Japanese] sent a PT boat after the pilot," Willard related. As the big Liberator readied to attack the boat and intervene on behalf of the downed fighter pilot, a US Navy submarine broke radio silence, and told the bomber to stay out of the fracas. As Willard watched in fascination, the submarine split the sea and surfaced, as deck gunners scrambled to get the range of the enemy boat. A few rounds from the sub's cannon was all it took to target the patrol boat and send it under. The pilot was plucked safely from the sea by the submarine.

Culminating Bill Willard's combat career was a mission over the decks of the USS *Missouri* on September 2, 1945, as the treaty ending World War II was being signed. "We took pictures of MacArthur and all of them right on the deck," Bill recalled with a gleam that cut through nearly five decades. Liberators saw the war begin, and they participated in a massive umbrella of airpower over the war's end in Tokyo Bay.

## Chapter 9

# No Higher Tribute:
# Liberator Crew Medals of Honor

If there's a hierarchy in aviation, pilots enjoy accolades beyond those bestowed on other aircrew members. In a 10-person B-24 roaring over a flak- and fighter-infested target, all are heroes, sometimes placed in harm's way by the decisive actions of a pilot who later is honored for his leadership of the crew under fire. The following is a complete list of AAF and Navy Liberator and Privateer fliers who received the Medal of Honor, America's highest tribute, for bravery. These recipients' individual acts of heroism should not be minimized, nor should the gallantry of the other nine crew members aboard their fated Liberators.

### Addison E. Baker

The cauldron of Ploesti yielded a group of Medals of Honor, conferred on fliers who steeled themselves to grim odds of survival, and pressed on stoically. Lt. Col. Addison E. Baker led the 93rd BG into the target area on the low-level mission of August 1, 1943. Oil refineries were at stake. Oil to fuel the Third Reich—and over which Germany would be forced to expend finite re-

*The restored B-24J* All American, *commemorating Liberator aviators, toured Tacoma, Washington, in June 1992. Frederick A. Johnsen*

sources defending against American attacks.

Addison Baker's dark olive-drab B-24D, blotched with medium green edging the wings and tail to hide the strikingly straight lines of the Liberator, sported the nickname *Hell's Wench.* It now carried an additional marking; the vertical fins sported British-style red-white-and-blue fin flashes, since the Americans were flying in skies defended by British gunners as they departed and returned to their North African airstrips. But mistaken identity and overzealous British gunners were far from Baker's thoughts as his B-24 roared to Ploesti at minimum altitude, to preserve surprise as long as possible.

Compound calamities and errors led mission navigators to remove their aircraft from the ponderous Ploesti formation before it cleared the Mediterranean. An overland error led the Liberators toward Bucharest, Romania, alerting more Axis defenses than necessary. Around Baker, his anxious 93rd BG watched as the formation headed in what many of them thought was the wrong direction. Baker made an eloquently simple decision as the smoke from Ploesti's stacks smudged the sky 90deg to the left. He turned *Hell's Wench* toward the refineries, breaking from the formation and taking the crews of his Traveling Circus, as the 93rd BG was nicknamed, directly to the target. Ploesti was not going as

planned, and Baker felt obliged to lead the Traveling Circus there, if no other bomb group made it. Some of the Circus' Liberators were down to 20ft above the Romanian countryside as phony haystacks toppled to expose antiaircraft guns. Turret gunners aboard the dark Liberators swapped fire with artillery troops on the ground. When they could, crew members glanced about, able to see pilots in other cockpits concentrating severely on flying, eyes straight ahead, as the big B-24s bucked in the wakes of the bombers ahead of them.

The Liberators screamed at 245mph, way in their emergency power setting range, and the crew wondered how long the Pratt & Whitneys could take the urgent abuse. A Traveling Circus bomber took a belting hit in its bomb bay; fire torched back behind the plane possibly three times its length. Few bailed out as the stricken plane's pilot traded airspeed for altitude to afford them the opportunity to jump. The flaming B-24 stalled and burned on the outskirts of a Romanian village as Addison Baker plowed ahead with the remaining members of the 93rd BG glued to his tail. Baker's heading was not as briefed because of the earlier mix-up in navigating. He and his copilot knew the group was dutifully roaring into battle right behind them, counting on their leadership to fill the vacuum left when one mission navigator crashed

*Unbelievable boiling pyres rose higher than the Liberators that caused them over Ploesti, Romania, on August 1, 1943. Courage, both documented and unnoticed, was demonstrated in the bucking B-24s that day.* US Air Force via Peter M. Bowers Collection

and his back-up dropped from formation.

Survivors of the low-level Ploesti mission reported seeing flak guns from 20 to 105mm in size. It was a large-bore gun, according to the citation for Addison Baker's Medal of Honor award, that fired the shell that punctured Baker's B-24 and set it afire, low over Romania. Only about three miles from the refinery complex when strick-en, Baker's Liberator was over wheat fields smooth enough to afford a reasonable chance of surviving a forced landing. Unwilling to leave his task before seeing it to completion, Baker ignored his own best chance for survival and held to his course, leading the 93rd BG to its refinery target. Others in the formation saw more than one hit on *Hell's Wench*. Still, Baker held course, leading his Traveling Circus toward the gap between two smokestacks over the refinery after clipping a barrage balloon cable that set the captive gas bag free. Crews in other Liberators reported the flight deck engulfed in flames; still *Hell's Wench* barreled ahead, on Addison Baker's determined course. Once the refinery was reached, *Hell's Wench* staggered for altitude, gaining about 300ft as some of the crew bailed out. Baker's bomber began falling off on its right wing tip, narrowly missing another B-24 before impacting the ground. None of his crew, including those who bailed out, survived Ploesti.

Addison Baker, while flying a B-24 Liberator, contributed a powerful lesson in selfless leadership that August day over Ploesti.

### John L. Jerstad

Maj. John L. Jerstad flew as Addison Baker's copilot in the 93rd BG B-24 nicknamed *Hell's Wench* over Ploesti's oil refineries on August 1, 1943. Former Missouri high school teacher Jerstad had enough missions behind him to avoid participation in Ploesti, but he volunteered to go. When Baker and Jerstad turned *Hell's Wench* and the rest of the 93rd BG toward the target area and away from the mistaken 376th BG's heading, *Hell's Wench* pointed the way over the heaviest antiaircraft defenses of the area. The heavy-bore hits on *Hell's Wench* appeared inevitable. Ploesti veterans from other Liberators have said they believe no one human could have held the stricken, flaming *Hell's Wench* on course for so long, adding evidence of Jerstad's contribution to the success of the mission. Major Jerstad's volunteerism was highlighted as a trait worthy of emulation, in the citation that posthumously gave him the Medal of Honor for his stoic heroics in a B-24D.

### Lloyd H. Hughes

Second Lt. Lloyd Hughes climbed into his 389th BG B-24D on August 1, 1943, and prepared for the impending inferno of Ploesti. The 389th's briefed Ploesti target refinery involved the longest flying of any of the sites the Liberators would hit. This Campina complex was also believed less heavily defended than some of the other refineries. The newer D-models of the 389th tanked more fuel than some of the earlier D-models of the other bomb groups. Extra weight, including ball turrets on some 389th Liberators, also made them slower than the others. So it was natural to send the longest-ranging Liberators to the farthest target refinery, and likewise logical to send these slower B-24s to the target with the lightest antiaircraft defenses.

But Campina was a blazing inferno by the time Hughes' B-24, part of the last formation, approached the target. Accurate groundfire punctured fuel tanks in the bomb bay and the left wing, sending gasoline spewing aft from the Liberator in dangerous streams. At this time, Hughes could have elected to leave formation, to afford his crew a chance to belly the bomber in, or possibly bail out. Ahead, flames from the damaged refinery leaped into the air higher than the altitude of Hughes' B-24.

Knowing the danger his leaking B-24 posed, Hughes held course and roared over the refinery. The gasoline fountain rushing from the B-24 ignited from the towering refinery fires, and other fliers saw Hughes finally attempt a forced landing after dropping his

bomb load. It was too late for landing; the rapidly developing fire consumed the Liberator, which crashed even as it appeared Hughes was trying, to the very end, to set it down in a river bed. Three men survived the crash; one of these died later. Hughes' posthumous Medal of Honor citation said he flew the Ploesti mission "motivated only by his high conception of duty which called for the destruction of his assigned target at any cost . . ."

### Leon W. Johnson

Col. Leon W. Johnson commanded the 44th BG, and led his group to Ploesti on August 1, 1943, from the copilot's seat of the B-24D nicknamed *Suzy-Q*. The 44th Group was part of the Ploesti armada that stretched out behind the leaders, falling farther back as Johnson decided to stay with the other lagging groups. A tedious frontal penetration over mountains at the border of Greece ate up more time for the 44th and the other trailing groups as they spread out to accommodate the lower altitude penetration through the clouds, required by some B-24s of the accompanying 98th BG which lacked oxygen for high altitude.

When some of the first B-24s neared the target area, while Leon Johnson's 44th BG was still distant, some wrong turns were made, and an impromptu salvaging of bomb runs saw another group hit Johnson's prearranged target refinery. Johnson's combat equation changed radically as antiaircraft gunners were primed by the earlier bombers overhead, and as delayed-fuze bombs from the earlier B-24s posed an imminent threat to the low-flying 44th BG, as did fires raging from the first Liberator attacks on Johnson's target. Intense smoke obscured parts of the refinery as Colonel Johnson led the way. The 44th was credited with totally destroying what remained of their target refinery in the Ploesti complex. Col. Leon Johnson survived to receive his Medal of Honor.

### John R. Kane

Col. John R. "Killer" Kane emerged from Ploesti, and North Africa, a figure in airpower folklore—the quintessential hard-driving group commander who led by example. His 98th BG, known as the Pyramiders, made North

Africa their backyard, even as they looked forward across the Mediterranean to an expanded war. Texan Kane earned his Medal of Honor on August 1, 1943, over Ploesti when he led the third, and largest, element of Liberators over the target. Part of the Ploesti force that was detained by weather en route, Kane's Pyramiders arrived over their assigned target only to find it had already been damaged by an earlier group gone astray. Kane faced gunners already practiced in tracking the low-flying Liberators of the first bomb group as they passed overhead. A train, packed with flak guns, audaciously ran along tracks parallel to the group's flight path, pouring fire into the low B-24s.

Kane's B-24D, nicknamed *Hail Columbia,* punched into boiling, flame-laced smoke clouds over the Astro Romana refinery. This was the single most important target of the Ploesti complex, now reeling from the delayed-action bombs of the earlier group who passed this way in the confusion of battle. Flak clunked into the No. 4 engine of *Hail Columbia,* and Kane feathered the prop. Bombs rippled out of the deep bays of his B-24, and Kane pressed on, as other Pyramiders less fortunate rode their desert-sand B-24s into the ground, slamming into the Astro Romana complex. Kane's Liberator would not make it back to Libya that day, limping as far as Cyprus before setting down out of necessity.

Operation Tidal Wave, the low-level Ploesti mission that swept over the Romanian countryside like a rolling wave, produced more Medals of Honor than any other single air action.

### Horace S. Carswell, Jr.

The Liberator's Pacific war frequently involved single-plane shipping strikes. On October 26, 1944, Maj. Horace S. Carswell, pilot, and his crew hoisted their B-24 into the sky and nosed out for the South China Sea, going it alone, at night. A convoy of 12 ships, shepherded by at least a pair of destroyers, steamed into the night oblivious to Carswell's approach. The trade-off was stark: Fly too high, and turning ships could wheel out of the way of falling bomb; fly too low, and risk death in withering antiaircraft fire thrown up by the ships. At 600ft, Car-

*Destined to earn the Medal of Honor in a B-24, Leon Vance held his daughter, Sharon D. Vance, beside the Liberator bearing her name, before he departed the United States for combat. Sharon D. Vance Kiernan Collection*

swell's heavy bomber made its first run unchallenged. A near miss was registered on one of the ships. Carswell circled for another pass over the now-alerted Japanese. The gauntlet was horrific. Even as the crew claimed two direct hits on a tanker, AA (antiaircraft) fire halted two of the B-24's engines and slowed the output of another. Carswell's copilot reeled from wounds. The B-24 sank toward the sea, hy-

draulics damaged and a gas tank holed. The citation honoring Major Carswell said he demonstrated a "magnificent display of flying skill" in checking the descent in the dark, and putting the B-24 into a faltering climb, chugging away from the convoy and toward the China coast. Landfall was a godsend for the crew, who could bail out and expect to survive this harrowing night. One man then learned the worst: His parachute was ripped by flak over the convoy, and was now a useless bundle of fabric.

Carswell's choices were few, and tough. While he ordered the rest of the crew to jump to safety, he remained at his seat in the cockpit, determined to crash-land the bomber in the dark if

need be to save his stranded crew member who had no parachute. The noble attempt ended abruptly against a mountainside, in a fireball. Major Carswell was honored for his selfless initiative with a posthumous Medal of Honor shortly after the end of the war. The Air Force further acknowledged Texan Horace Carswell by naming Carswell AFB in Fort Worth after this native son.

## Leon R. Vance, Jr.

Oklahoman Leon Vance is remembered as a big man who embraced life with gusto, excelling in athletics and enjoying a hard-driving poker game. In wartime interviews, he showed a soft facet to his character, proudly naming his B-24H after two-year-old daughter Sharon Drury Vance. But it was not in his beloved *Sharon D.* that Lt. Col. Leon Vance would earn the Medal of Honor.

On June 5, 1944, in preparation for the D-day invasion, Vance led the 489th BG against coastal positions near Wimereaux, France. The mission was part of the choreography intended to keep the Germans guessing where the invasion would land. As mission commander, Vance stood on the wide Liberator flight deck behind and between the pilot's and copilot's seats. The route in to Wimereaux was devoid of German fighters, but filled with antiaircraft fire. Vance counted just 10sec to the target gun emplacements when accurate flak knocked out three of the B-24H's engines. The olive-drab Liberator struggled on, leading the 489th successfully to the drop on one engine. Fateful flak then exploded just outside the cockpit of the B-24, killing the pilot and almost cutting off Vance's right foot. It was hopeless to try to hold formation in a damaged Liberator with only one engine, and a ragged right elevator.

While the copilot flew the Liberator, another crewman constricted a tourniquet around Vance's leg above the nearly severed foot. Crew members raced to stave off fuel leaks, purging gasoline through the open bomb bay doors. More flak rocked the doomed Liberator. The battered bomber continually lost altitude on its return journey across the English Channel, and Vance struggled to fly the aircraft from the floor near the copilot's seat, and ordered the rest of the crew to bail out over England. By now, the Liberator was descending through 12,000ft in a pure glide; the last of the Pratt & Whitneys was dead, but windmilling, unable to feather.

Vance did not assess the gravity of his wounds at the moment. His grievously injured foot, still attached to his leg, was entangled in armor plating, preventing him from getting up from the cockpit floor. "I couldn't take my hands off the controls to get my leg loose, because the ship would have stalled," he recalled later in a hospital in England. Lying on his stomach to reach the control wheel, Vance heard intercom chatter that led him to believe his wounded radio operator remained in the waist of the Liberator, unable to bail out. In fact, other crew members assisted the injured man in jumping from the descending bomber. Now Vance prepared to ditch the Liberator in the sea, the safest of the poor options available to the crippled flier. Like the competitor he was, Leon Vance kept thinking, devising, and performing in the best interests of his crew and himself all the way down, never resigning himself to an uncontrolled crash, despite his own dire predicament.

Vance used his parachute pack as padding to prevent head and neck injuries from the shock of ditching deceleration. Impact with the water tore the Martin top turret loose, and several hundred pounds of armored gun turret hurled forward to pin Colonel Vance in the cockpit. "It was lying across my back, and I was under about six feet of water," Vance recalled. "I figured that was the end of the line for me." Vance held his breath as he performed what he acknowledged was an odd act: He released the safety harness of the dead pilot beside him. Just as Vance felt his lungs would burst, something within the Liberator exploded and hurled him, amputated from his right foot, to the surface. He dragged himself over the wreckage in an attempt to reach the waist where he still believed his radio operator was trapped, but at last Leon Vance's heroic strength gave out. Marshaling just enough energy to pull the lanyards allowing his Mae West life preserver to inflate with carbon dioxide gas, Vance was in the water when a British rescue boat snatched him some 50min later.

Vance convalesced well in England, and was dispatched back to the United States late in July aboard a Douglas C-54 Skymaster transport that was lost en route. Vance AFB in Oklahoma was named in his honor.

### Bruce Avery Van Voorhis

Hailing from the lumber port town of Aberdeen, Washington, Bruce Van Voorhis joined the Navy in Nevada. He commanded Navy squadron VPB-102 on July 6, 1943, during the battle for the Solomon Islands. As a PB4Y-1 plane commander, Van Voorhis volunteered for a risky single-ship bombing mission against a Japanese installation on Greenwich Island. Urgency attended the mission, deemed vital to staving off a Japanese attack of American positions.

Van Voorhis launched his Liberator in darkness, without escort, on the 700mi journey to Greenwich. Winds varied capriciously en route; visibility was low and terrain treacherous as Van Voorhis wended his way to the enemy installation, which he reached to the accompaniment of antiaircraft bursts blooming around his PB4Y-1. As Japanese warplanes engaged the Liberator in combat, one was shot down. The enemy planes caused Van Voorhis to seek the relative safety of lower altitude, which denied the fighters three-dimensional freedom to execute sweeping attacks. The Navy flier set up six attacks on the base, and was credited with destroying the vital radio installation on Greenwich, as well as other facilities and three more enemy aircraft—seaplanes on the water. It was the blast from his own bombs that felled Van Voorhis' low-skimming Liberator. His mission was a sacrificial bid to thwart the enemy; against incredible odds, his chance of survival was dubious. He died in the wreck of his PB4Y-1, and the Navy singled out Lt. Comdr. Bruce Avery Van Voorhis as the only Liberator or Privateer airman in their service to earn the Medal of Honor.

### Donald D. Pucket

Donald D. Pucket flew a 98th Bomb Group B-24 on a high-level bombing run over Ploesti on June 9, 1944, when flak rocked the Liberator. Handing the bomber over to the copilot, Lieutenant Pucket tended wounded crew members first, and then assessed the condition of the damaged B-24. With two engines producing power, chances of returning home were poor, so Pucket called for the crew to abandon the bomber. Because three of the men aboard could not bail out, Lieutenant Pucket stayed with them and tried to fly the crippled Liberator to a crash landing. A third engine stopped, and the bomber crashed. For his selflessness, Donald Pucket was posthumously awarded the Medal of Honor.

# Liberator and Privateer Training Bases

The following list represents sites in the United States where some aspect of training involving Liberators or Privateers took place at some period during World War II. Training missions changed during the war; Army airfields like Ephrata and Walla Walla, Washington, at various times hosted B-17s and B-24s. Due to the ever-changing training doctrine during the war, this list may not reflect every site where B-24s were employed in training, but it represents a core of that effort.

Alamogordo AAF, New Mexico
Barksdale AAB, Louisiana
Biggs AAF, Texas
Bruning AAF, Nebraska
Camp Kearney, California (US Navy)
Clovis AAB, New Mexico
Davis-Monthan AAF, Arizona
Ephrata AAF, Washington
Fort Myers, Florida
Gowen AAF, Idaho
Kearns AAF, Utah
Liberal AAF, Kansas
Lowry AAB, Colorado

March AAF, California
McCook AAF, Nebraska
MacDill AAF, Florida
Mountain Home AAB, Idaho
Muroc AAF, California
Pocatello AAF, Idaho
Pueblo AAF, Colorado
Salt Lake City AAB, Utah
Sioux City AAB, Iowa
Tonopah AAF, Nevada
Walla Walla AAB, Washington
Wendover AAF, Utah

# Descriptive Bibliography

Much has been written about the B-24—the most-produced American warplane. The following bibliography goes beyond titles and publishers to characterize the nature of these volumes. Some are out of print. They all contribute something to the fabric of the Liberator story—a story too vast for any one book to encompass.

Arnold, Rhodes. *The B-24/PB4Y in Combat—The World's Greatest Bomber.* Reserve, New Mexico: Pima Paisano Publications, circa 1990.

One of the staunchest defenders of the B-24, Arnold played a role in acquiring and flying a B-24J from India to Tucson, Arizona, in 1969 for the Pima Air Museum. Arnold's unabashedly pro-Liberator book is significant for its detailed treatment of Eleventh AF operations, and its table of combat losses that may help other historians unravel the fates of lost Liberators. Arnold also incorporated a list of Liberator nose art names, matched to s/ns or units wherever known. This isn't a beginner's B-24 book, or a sweeping Liberator biography to answer all questions about the bomber. But it is a delightfully quirky addition to any serious B-24 historian's bookshelf.

Birdsall, Steve. *Log of the Liberators.* New York: Doubleday, 1973.

Here's a good one for the human-interest side of the B-24 story. Birdsall blended his crew narratives with just enough AAF and Navy history to flesh out a readable biography of the Liberator. Not too technical; very personal and personable.

———. *The B-24 Liberator.* New York: Arco, 1968.

The old Arco Famous Aircraft series of softbound books filled a need in the 1960s for inexpensive, photo-laden reference works on planes including the Liberator. Birdsall marshaled a good group of photos, coupled with his trademark—human-interest narratives about the men who served in B-24s. Birdsall did not set out to write a nuts-and-bolts B-24 book with this volume; he did create a very readable set of vignettes.

Blue, Allan G. *The B-24 Liberator.* New York: Charles Scribner's Sons, 1975.

Allan Blue's hardback biography of the B-24 is a must-read. Blue goes into great detail on construction changes and modifications, and demystifies some Liberator myths and question marks. Includes capsule histories of numerous Liberator combat units, and contains many tables and appendices of production data and serials.

Bowman, Martin. *The B-24 Liberator, 1939–1945.* Norwich, England: Wensum Books, 1979.

Bowman's book is at its best when treating crew reminiscences anecdotally, and when covering British and Commonwealth Liberators—this book gives an interesting view from across the pond.

Davis, Larry. *B-24 Liberator in Action.* Carrollton, Texas: Squadron-Signal Publications, 1987.

Number eighty in the ongoing line of Squadron-Signal aircraft monographs, Larry Davis' effort is an easy-to-use reference when building a B-24 or PB4Y model. A cache of photos and some generally well-executed color renderings by Don Greer make this an inexpensive addition to a B-24 library.

# Index